Contents

1 Young heroes

Read this section of 'Kara's one big chance'.

The hall is silent, listening. "Fishing *is* the heart of this town." I look around. This is my one big chance.

"The boat my mum and dad rebuilt together, fished from this harbour a hundred years ago. Back then, she would have come home so full the fish would have been spilling over her sides into the sea." I swallow hard. The back of my throat is dry. I look around and fix my eye on Dougie Evans. "But she can't do that anymore. We've taken all the fish from our seas. Dougie Evans's **trawlers** have to go further and deeper to find fish, and even then they sometimes come back empty. Now we're tearing up the **reef**. I wonder, will we still be fishing here at all in another hundred years?" I glance across the hall. There's no sign of Felix, but I remember what he wanted me to say. "You're about to see what we could lose."

I stand there in the silence and look around the hall. I don't know what's meant to happen now. I climb down the steps and sit next to Dad.

The hall lights go out.

I hear Mum, speaking through the darkness.

The room is silent. The huge screen on the stage is dark at first. A faint greenish glow in the centre of the screen becomes brighter and brighter and we are rising up, towards the sun shining through the surface of the water. A seal swims up to the camera. It's as if he's watching everyone in the hall. His big dog eyes are chocolate brown. Silver bubbles spiral upwards and he twists away, his grey body sliding through the water.

A　**1** Who is Kara speaking to? _____

　　2 Why is she speaking to them? _____

　　3 Explain the change which has taken place in the sea. _____

　　_____

　　4 The writer uses a short sentence which is also a one-line paragraph in the middle of the text. Why? What effect does it have?

　　_____

　　_____

B　Rewrite the extract from a different point of view. You are the fisherman Dougie Evans sitting in the audience. You've come to hear Kara talk as well as defend your right to fish in the sea.

_____

_____

_____

_____

_____

_____

_____

_____

_____

_____

_____

Sentence length and the use of 'and'

Rewrite the story using both long and short sentences and extra vocabulary to create tension. Instead of reported speech, use direct speech. Don't forget to start the dialogue on a new line and to use appropriate punctuation.

So, Kam and I were completely lost, in the middle of this huge forest and we knew it was bear territory and night time was already falling, so we huddled up together, under a tree to keep warm and then suddenly Kam asked me what that noise was and I said that I didn't know what it was and then she said it was something really big and it sounded like it was coming towards us and I agreed with her and she said that whatever it was, it was getting closer and closer and she was sounding pretty scared by this time and I was beginning to feel a bit worried too I didn't know what to do and then I saw two horrible, white eyes coming closer and closer and closer I thought just then I was about to scream and then I saw that it was my dad and big brother, with torches, looking for us.

Main and subordinate clauses

Linking clauses to make multi-clause sentences

A Choose an appropriate **clause** from a–f to turn the clauses 1–6 into complete sentences.

1 This is the girl   **a** when I spilt my drink all over myself.

2 I wish I knew   **b** if it snows a lot this winter.

3 My mum asked me   **c** since he was six years old.

4 I was so embarrassed   **d** who I was telling you about.

5 I will learn to ski   **e** why I had not eaten my lunch.

6 He has known Annul   **f** where I left my book.

B Rewrite the following sentences, missing out the **subordinating conjunction** and making any necessary changes to the **verb**. The first one has been done for you.

1 At the zoo, I saw an elephant which was eating a banana.

At the zoo, I saw an elephant eating a banana.

2 The girl who was sitting next to me in the exam couldn't find her pencil.

3 The yellow car that is parked outside belongs to my neighbour's son.

4 I have seen the film, which is showing at the local cinema, three times.

Direct speech

Appropriate language and punctuation

A **Read this short passage. Add all the missing punctuation, including exclamation and question marks. Then replace each instance of the word 'said' with a more descriptive and powerful verb.**

Oh no what was that terrible noise said (_____) Omar

There's going to be an avalanche said (_____) Daniel

Quick hurry as fast as you can Quicker Quicker Hurry up You must get to the side away from the avalanche said (_____) Omar

I can't I can't make it It's coming too quickly said (_____) Daniel

Move said (_____) Omar

I'm going too slowly said (_____) Daniel Omar I can't... the snow is ... said (_____) Daniel

Just do it said (_____) Omar Quickly grab hold of my ski pole I'm aiming for that large rock over there

I've got it I've got it just go go go said (_____) Daniel

Made it Wow look at that That's amazing said (_____) Omar A few minutes later Omar gave Daniel a friendly slap on the back and said (_____) It's alright the danger has passed. Are you OK

Yeah that was a close one though said (_____) Daniel

B Now write your own dialogue between two people caught in a hurricane together. Try to use really dramatic language to make it exciting and remember to punctuate your dialogue correctly.

_____

_____

_____

_____

_____

_____

_____

_____

_____

_____

_____

_____

_____

_____

_____

Colons and semicolons

When to use colons and semicolons

A Add the correct punctuation to the following sentences.

1 A number of children still need to bring in their signed permission slips before they can go on the school trip Hiroto Dana Nathan Abdul Arjun and Teodora

2 You will need to bring in seven ingredients to make the fairy cakes flour sugar butter eggs milk icing sugar and chocolate buttons

3 He had a lot of things on his birthday wish list a new computer game an art set a book a scooter a mobile phone with earphones to play music and a tin of sweets

B Connect the following sentences by using a semicolon and making the appropriate adjustments.

1 Some people like to eat breakfast as soon as they get up. Other people are unable to eat until they've been awake for a couple of hours.

2 Many people dislike jogging in the rain and getting wet. Personally, I find it very enjoyable.

3 Leo hadn't realised that his brother had left his wet painting on the seat when he sat down. Now his new trousers were ruined.

C Write two sentences of your own using a colon.

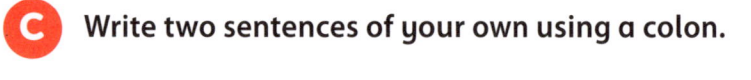

Write two sentences of your own using a semicolon.

Check my learning

Unit 1 Young heroes

Name _____

Date _____

☺ I understand and I can do this well.

😐 I understand, but I am not confident.

☹ I don't understand and this is difficult.

Learning objective	☺	😐	☹
Reading skills			
I can begin to show awareness of writers' choices of sentence length and structure.			
I can identify uses of colons and semicolons.			
I can identify direct speech.			
Writing skills			
I can use correct grammar in multi-clause sentences.			
I can punctuate speech and use apostrophes accurately.			
I can identify the main clause and other clauses in a multi-clause sentence.			
I can use punctuation effectively to show the meaning in multi-clause sentences.			
I can write from a different narrative viewpoint.			
I can develop imaginative detail through careful use of vocabulary.			

I would like more help with _____

_____

_____

(2) Health and sport

Biography

Name: Sadio Mané

Birthday: 10 April, 1992

Nationality: Senegalese

Place of birth: Sédhiou (grew up in the small village of Bambali)

Position: Midfielder

Club: Premier League Club Liverpool and the Senegal national team

Inspiration: Inspired to pursue a career in football after he saw his country's team reach the quarter-finals at the 2002 World Cup

Previous clubs: French club: Metz; Austrian club: Red Bull Salzburg; English club: Southampton

Facts:

- He transferred to Liverpool for £37 million, making him the most expensive African player of that time.

- Mané also played for the Senegalese national team, helping them reach the quarter-finals in the 2012 Olympics.

- He holds a world record for the fastest hat-trick in 2 minutes and 56 seconds.

- He donates a lot of money to charity. For example, he donated £200,000 to a school in Senegal and £41,000 to the health system.

A Read the profile of young footballer Sadio Mané.

1 Use the information to write a short biography of Sadio Mané. You could do some research and add additional information if you like.

2 Research a sports person who you admire and/or is popular in your country. Write a short biography about them. Say when they were born, where they grew up, what they have achieved and what you think they might want to achieve in the future.

Adverbials of time

A Use the **adverbials of time** in the box to complete the instructions to make a sponge cake.

At the same time	Secondly	then	First	After that
Once that's done	Next	and then	Finally	

Sponge cake method

_____, line a tin with baking parchment. _____, ask an adult to turn the oven on to 180° C. _____, grate the carrots on the fine side of the grater, _____ tip them into a large bowl.

_____, sift the sugar, flour, bicarbonate of soda and cinnamon into the bowl with the carrot. _____, add the orange zest and mix everything up.

_____, break the eggs into a bowl (scoop out any bits of shell),

_____ add them to the other bowl along with the oil. Mix everything together thoroughly.

_____, scoop the cake mix into your tin and level the top. Ask an adult to put it in the oven for 30 minutes or until the cake is cooked. Let it cool.

B Add your own adverbials of time to complete the instructions for the icing.

To make the icing, _____ mix the butter and icing sugar together,

_____ stir in the soft cheese until smooth. _____, spread the icing over the cooled cake. _____, decorate with sprinkles, if you like.

Using the right words

Read this article from a school newspaper.

Usain Bolt, nicknamed 'Lightning Bolt', is perhaps one of the most naturally gifted athletes the world has ever seen. Regarded by some as the fastest man on Earth ever, Bolt confirmed his unique talent by winning gold in the
5   100m, 200m and the 4×100m at the 2015 World Championships in Beijing.

Usain Bolt was born on 21st August 1986 in Jamaica, where he grew up. As a young child, he spent most of his time playing cricket and football. He discovered a talent for running when he started school but it took a while before he took his talent seriously.

10   By the age of 15, the young Usain was nearly two metres in height and he completely dominated the 2002 World Junior Championships. He was the youngest person ever to win the 200m race and was a member of the teams who set a new record in the 4×100m relay and the 4×400m relay.

At the age of 17, he signed his first professional contract. At the 2003
15   CARIFTA games, he won gold medals, but a leg injury meant that Usain didn't perform well in the 2004 summer games in Athens. By 2007, he was recovered and won silver at the World Championships. But it was at the 2008 Olympics that Usain Bolt became a household name.

Usain Bolt took the 2008 Olympics in Beijing by storm. He won three gold
20   medals and broke three world records. He became the first man in history to win both the 100m and 200m races in world record times, and broke a world record with the 4x100m team..

He maintained his legendary status in the 2012 Olympic Games in London by defending all three of his Olympic titles and again being part of the team
25   that set a new world record in the 4×100m relay.

In 2015, despite a year of injuries, Usain Bolt defended all three of his titles at the World Championships in Beijing.

Comprehension

A **1** What nickname is Usain sometimes given?

_____

2 How did Usain 'dominate' the 2002 World Junior Championships?

_____

3 Why was it quite surprising that he did so well in the 2015 games?

_____

B **Using information from the text, answer the following questions.**

1 Match each of the subheadings below to the text on page 14. Write each subheading on the correct line in the text.

The Olympics **Lightning Bolt!** **Defending his titles** **Growing up**

2 What is the purpose of subheadings in a text like this?

_____

3 This text is a short biography. List five general features of a biography.

_____

_____

_____

_____

C **1** Find a synonym for the following words in the first paragraph of the text.

thought of _____ exclusive _____ talented _____

2 Usain Bolt <u>took</u> the 2008 Olympics <u>by storm</u>. To take something 'by storm' is an idiom. What do you think it means?

_____

_____

Prefixes and suffixes

Defining words

A Match the words with a **prefix** or a **suffix** (1–5) with their definitions (a–e).

1 meaning**ful**

2 **un**pack

3 **re**form

4 **mis**interpret

5 **fore**father

a ancestor

b full of significance, purpose or value

c to not understand correctly

d to remove the contents

e to form again

> • -ful means 'full of'
> • re- means 'again' or 'back'
> • mis- means 'wrong'

B Choose a **root word** from the list below and add a prefix or a suffix from the clouds. Then match the new word to its definition below.

cover   help   colour   comfort   response

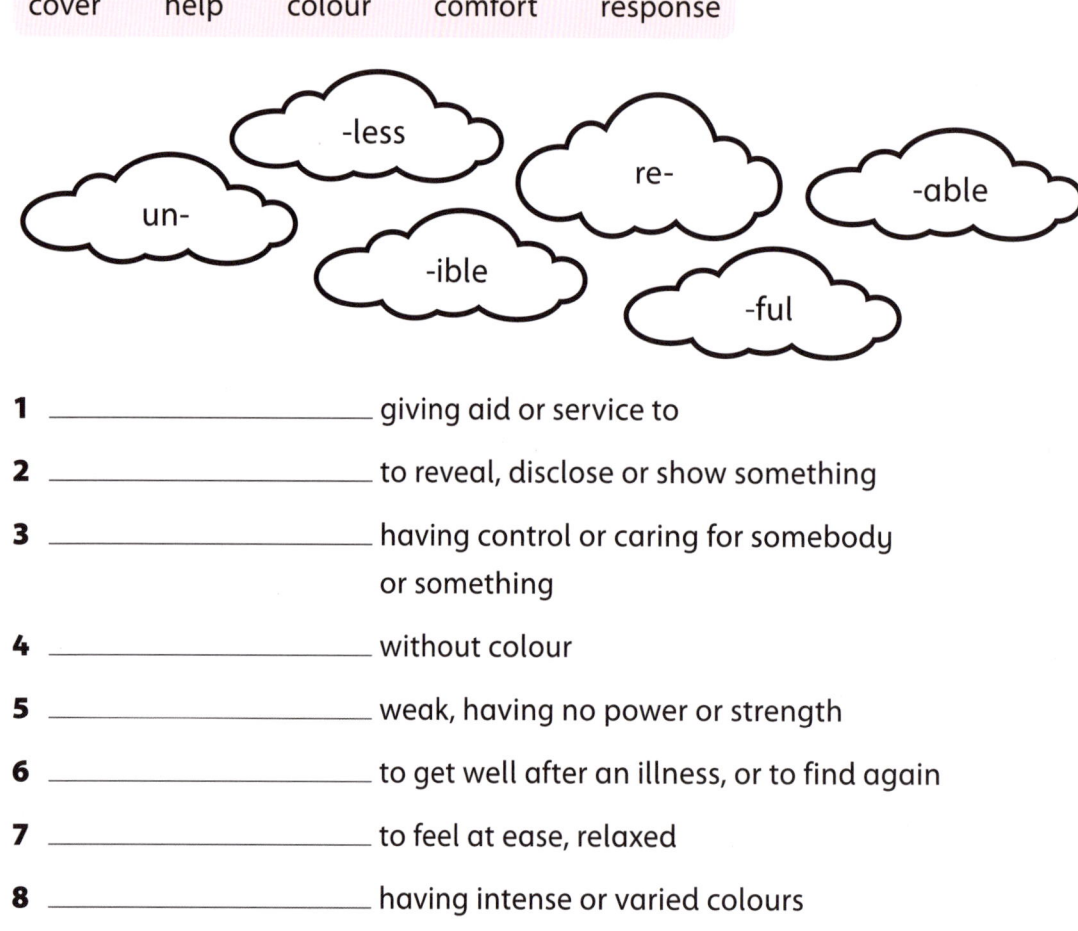

-less
re-
-able
un-
-ible
-ful

1 _____ giving aid or service to

2 _____ to reveal, disclose or show something

3 _____ having control or caring for somebody
   or something

4 _____ without colour

5 _____ weak, having no power or strength

6 _____ to get well after an illness, or to find again

7 _____ to feel at ease, relaxed

8 _____ having intense or varied colours

Single clause and multi-clause sentences

Working with different kinds of sentence

A Complete these **single clause** sentences with an appropriate verb.

1 I _____ my toes lightly in the cool, shimmering water.

2 It _____ great news!

3 She _____ the book on the table.

4 Yesterday, they _____ on holiday for two weeks.

B Decide whether the following sentences are single clause or **multi-clause**.

1 I like Eddy, but sometimes he's a bit silly.

_____

2 It's quite late so, if you want to get up early, you should go to bed now.

_____

3 The six beautiful brown and black hens in the garden lay an egg each, every day.

_____

_____

C Write three sentences about what you will do tomorrow. Make one single clause sentence, one with a main clause and a subordinate clause and one with two main clauses.

Single clause _____

_____

Main and subordinate clause _____

_____

Two main clauses _____

_____

Fact or opinion

Read the extract from Mike Perham's autobiography.

Panic is not something I normally associate with the ocean. It's where I feel most at home. Its uncontrollable dangers are part of the life of a sailor like me.

I **wedged** myself inside the cabin, at the chart table, which was the safest place to be. I tried to work on the chart. It gave me something to do instead of just worrying about the conditions, which were **forecast** to continue for at least another twenty-four hours. Everything else was soaking wet but I was okay.

The **freak** wave that came thundering through the darkness must have been enormous. Hiding away in the cabin, I didn't see it coming but I had a one-minute warning. Its **deafening** roar! It scooped the boat up and **slammed** it flat on its side in an instant. Helpless, all I could do was hold my breath and **somersault** with the boat. The fear that hit me was instant. The noise was ridiculous; the boat creaked, groaned, rattled and screamed.

A Read the following statements and say whether they are fact or opinion.

1 The rain was expected to last for 24 hours. _____

2 Mike Perham tried to secure himself by squeezing into a small space. _____

3 The freak wave made the loudest sound ever. _____

4 Mike Perham is calmer than other people when he is sailing. _____

5 The boat was pushed on its side by the 'freak' wave. _____

B Explain how the writer emphasises the noise of the 'freak wave'.
Give **three** ways.

_____

_____

_____

C Write a paragraph about a true or imaginary time when you were in great danger. Try to build up the tension until the end of the paragraph when finally everything is OK.

Check my learning

Unit 2 Health and sport

Name _____

Date _____

😊 I understand and I can do this well.

😐 I understand, but I am not confident.

☹ I don't understand and this is difficult.

Learning objective	😊	😐	☹
Reading skills			
I can recognise the key features of biographies.			
I can compare the language and style of biographies.			
I can tell the difference between fact and opinion.			
Writing skills			
I can use prefixes and suffixes in my writing.			
I can write single and multi-clause sentences.			
I know how to select appropriate styles of non-fiction to influence my own writing.			
I can use adverbials of time in my writing.			

I would like more help with _____

_____

_____

_____

3 Stormy weather

Character profiles

A Look at the characters below. Make notes on what they look like and then describe what you think their character is like.

Prospero

_____

_____

_____

_____

_____

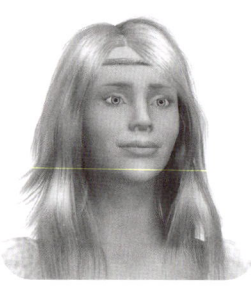

Miranda

_____

_____

_____

_____

_____

Antonio

_____

_____

_____

_____

_____

Ariel

_____

_____

_____

_____

_____

B **Read the text below which describes the appearance of Ariel in the forest.**

King Alonso, Antonio and a group of noblemen are making their way through thick **undergrowth**. There is the sound of chattering, shrieking monkeys in the trees overhead and the squawking of parrots. The men are exhausted and terribly thirsty and hungry. King Alonso is calling out for Ferdinand.

They come to a clearing with a huge table, and it is at this point that strange, **melancholic** music fills the forest and a **procession** of creatures in different, **bizarre** forms slips through the trees, bringing a **banquet** of delicious food. The animals dance about the table, invite the king and his party to eat, and then dance away. The men disagree at first about whether to eat or not. Just as the men are about to eat, however, thunder erupts, and Ariel appears in the shape of a bird.

Ariel claps his wings upon the table and the banquet vanishes. He ridicules the men for trying to draw their swords, which have been made to feel strangely heavy. Calling himself the image of **Destiny**, he goes on to accuse Alonso and Antonio of wrongly **banishing** Prospero from Milan and leaving him and his little girl at the mercy of the sea. For this sin, he tells them, nature and the sea have taken revenge on Alonso by taking Ferdinand. Ariel vanishes, and the creatures enter again and remove the banquet table.

C Complete the scene from the play where Ariel appears in front of King Alonso and Antonio disguised as a giant bird. Use the text from page 21 to help you.

Act I, Scene III

Thick undergrowth on the left-hand side of the stage with the sound of chattering, shrieking monkeys in the trees overhead and other noises including the squawking of parrots. On the right side of the stage is a clearing with a huge table. Enter King Alonso, Antonio and a small group of noblemen through the undergrowth, looking exhausted and using branches to swat flies.

KING ALONSO	Ferdinand, Ferdinand, oh my noble son, where are you?
ANTONIO	(quietly imitating Alonso so he can't hear) 'Ferdinand, oh dear sweet Ferdinand ...'
FIRST NOBLEMAN	What! What on earth is a table doing here?
ANTONIO	Wow! That's weird.

Soft melancholy music begins to play and gets louder.

KING ALONSO   Where is that music coming from?

_____

_____

_____

_____

_____

_____

_____

_____

_____

_____

Words, old and new

Many common English words were originally adapted from other languages.

A Match each word (1–6) with the word it is related to (a–f).

1	quarrel	**a**	from the Chinese word *kéjāp*
2	story	**b**	from the French word *carotte*
3	hero	**c**	from the Latin word *factum*
4	fact	**d**	from the Latin word *historia*
5	carrot	**e**	from the Medieval word *quadrellus*
6	ketchup	**f**	from the Greek word *hérōs*

B Match each word (1–9) with the the country of its origins (a–i).

1	democracy	**a**	Italy (from *concerto*)
2	homonym	**b**	Italy (from *opera* meaning work, action)
3	telephone	**c**	Spain (from *brisa* meaning cold, northeast wind)
4	feast	**d**	Greece (from *demos* meaning people)
5	concert	**e**	Italy (from *sŏlus* meaning alone)
6	opera	**f**	Spain (from *huracán*)
7	solo	**g**	Greece (from *homos* meaning same)
8	breeze	**h**	Greece (from *phone* meaning sound)
9	hurricane	**i**	France (from *feste* with the same meaning)

C Choose two words from the list below and write two definitions for each. Write one definition of the word's present meaning and one definition of what it used to mean. Use an online dictionary to help you.

stupid	doom	bully	nervous	sad	pretty	guy	evil	nice

_____

_____

_____

_____

Modal verbs

Modal verbs are used to indicate how sure the writer is that something happened, is happening or will happen, using verbs like could, might, or will.

A **Complete these sentences about yourself.**

1 If I were older, I might _____

2 If I were much taller, I could _____

3 If I were very rich, I could _____

4 If I were a bird, I would _____

B **Complete these sentences with a suitable modal verb.**

must	might	can't	would	can

1 You _____ go in there because it's not allowed.

2 She said she _____ definitely play tennis with me when it stopped raining.

3 _____ I borrow a pencil, please? I've lost mine.

4 There are a lot of clouds in the sky, so it _____ rain this afternoon.

5 You _____ wipe your shoes or you will not be allowed in.

C **Write your own sentences using the following modal verbs.**

won't _____

will _____

should _____

shall _____

cannot _____

A **Read the text below.**

ARIEL	The ship is here, master Prospero.
PROSPERO	Good work Ariel, it is time to say goodbye. Give us a good wind back to Milan. Enjoy the island my dear, loyal friend – I shall remember you always.
ARIEL	Goodbye and good luck, fine Prospero.

(Prospero turns to smile at Ariel but he has already disappeared. Prospero turns to look around – the island is in sunshine now, but still littered with leaves and branches from the storm. Monkeys and birds are flitting through the trees.)

PROSPERO	Hmm. Finally, I am leaving the island to return home … as Duke of Milan once again.

(And with those words Prospero turns to King Alonso.)

PROSPERO	Come, Alonso. All's well that ends well. We have much to catch up on.

(Prospero turns and exits with Alonso, followed by Miranda and Ferdinand. Only Antonio is left on the stage.)

ANTONIO	*(pulling a grimace, talking directly to the audience in a whining, mocking voice)* 'All's well that ends well'. Hmph! Welcome back, big brother!

B **Is Prospero happy to be leaving the island? Give evidence from the text.**

_____

_____

_____

C **How does Antonio feel about his brother's return to Milan? Do you think Antonio has any regrets about banishing his brother many years ago?**

_____

Commas, brackets and dashes

A Put commas in the correct places in the following sentences.

1 Tigers which were almost extinct only 10 years ago may now have a brighter future.

2 She hugged her teddy a present from her auntie and fell asleep.

3 His granny lived on Arran an island on the west coast of Scotland so he didn't see her very often.

4 The airplane which was very hot and crowded took off an hour late.

5 She had a picture by Hunderwasser the famous artist on her wall.

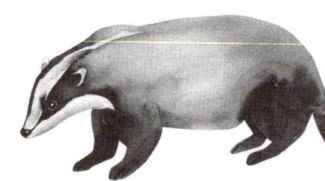

B Rewrite these sentences, by taking the extra information out of the brackets and adding it to the sentence at a suitable point. Don't forget to use commas.

1 Badgers eat berries, worms and small rodents. (found across Europe)

_____

2 Bao loves reading books by Shen Shixi but always cries at the sad endings. (a popular Chinese author)

_____

3 Zimbabwe is known for its amazing wildlife. (a landlocked country)

_____

C Rewrite these sentences, placing the extra information in brackets at a suitable point in the sentence. Use brackets, commas or dashes to separate the phrase or clause you have added.

1 The fourth Harry Potter film is on the TV tonight. (the best film ever)

_____

2 Phil Foden plays for Manchester City. (born 28 May 2000)

_____

3 Sebastian is the twin brother of Viola. (who is getting married to Olivia) (also known as Cesario)

_____

Check my learning

Unit 3 Stormy weather

Name _____

Date _____

☺ I understand and I can do this well.

😐 I understand, but I am not confident.

☹ I don't understand and this is difficult.

Learning objective	☺	😐	☹
Reading skills			
I have developed familiarity with an established author – Shakespeare.			
I can comment on a writer's use of language.			
I can read a text and answer comprehension questions.			
I can build up an idea of characters from what I read.			
Writing skills			
I can develop some imaginative detail through careful use of vocabulary.			
I can adapt the conventions of a text type for a particular purpose, i.e. to write a playscript.			
I can write character profiles.			

I would like more help with _____

_____

_____

_____

(4) Traditional tales and fables

Vocabulary

Read this traditional tale from South America.

In the Andes Mountains of Ecuador there once lived two great friends, the Clouds and Forest. They were such good friends that they would be completely absorbed by each
5   other for weeks and weeks on end. One day, however, they had a <u>squabble</u>, which turned into rather an unpleasant row and soon got completely out of hand. There was such an air of <u>hostility</u> between the old friends that
10 neither would **back down**. The Clouds decided to go somewhere else and Forest decided to focus on expanding its size.

But the animals and birds of the forest were miserable that the two friends had **fallen out** because their lives depended on the Clouds and
15 Forest being together. They thought of a <u>cunning</u> plan **to get** the two friends **back together**. The great condor wrote a <u>charming</u> apology letter and flew to the Clouds with it, saying it was from Forest. Meanwhile, the anaconda gave a copy of the same letter to Forest, but signed it from the Clouds. However, neither the Clouds nor Forest were fooled by the
20 letters. They both **saw through** the trick straight away and <u>scolded</u> the animals severely.

Seeing their plan fail, the unhappy animals and birds prepared to leave the forest and look for somewhere else to live. That night, the forest was very quiet. But the next morning all the animals were really
25 surprised to see the Cloud and Forest had got back together, acting as if nothing had ever come between them. Surprised, the condor, anaconda and other animals went and asked the two friends why they had **made up** again. With a smile, the friends explained that the animals' letters made them realise just how well they knew each other, and also what
30 their friendship meant, not just to them, but also to others around them.

28

Comprehension

A   **1** Who were good friends? _____

2 What happened that made them stop being friends?

_____

3 Who was affected by the breakup of their friendship?

_____

4 How did those who were affected by the breakup try to get them to be friends again?

_____

_____

5 Choose the best moral for this story.

   a Think about others before you think about yourself.

   b True friends are hard to find so when you find them, keep them.

   c Treat others as you want to be treated yourself.

B   **1** Some of the words are underlined in the text. Match those words with a synonym listed below.

disagreement _____   lovely _____   bad feeling _____

clever _____   told off _____

2 Explain what 'out of hand' means (line 8).

C   **Find the following phrasal verbs (in bold) in the text and use the context to explain their meaning.**

• to back down _____

• to fall out _____

• to get back together _____

• to see through _____

• to make up _____

Word classes

The Ant and the Dove

<u>An</u> ant went to the <u>bank</u> of a river to <u>drink</u>, but she fell in and <u>was carried</u> away by the rush of the water. She was on the point of <u>drowning</u>. A dove sitting on a tree <u>over</u> the water plucked a leaf <u>and</u> let <u>it</u> fall into the stream <u>close</u> to her. The ant climbed <u>onto</u> it and floated to <u>the</u> bank <u>safely</u>.

    <u>Shortly afterwards</u>, a hunter came and laid a trap for the dove under the tree. The ant, seeing what he wanted to do, <u>stung</u> the hunter on the foot. The hunter let out a cry of <u>pain</u> and the noise made the dove fly away.

 A Look at the underlined words and phrases in the text. Use the words in the box to complete the table with the correct word class. Two words have been done for you.

> abstract noun   passive verb form   adverb   irregular past tense   noun
> co-ordinating conjunction   ~~definite article~~   adjective   present participle
> preposition   adverbial of time   ~~indefinite article~~   pronoun   infinitive verb

Example from text	Word class	Example from text	Word class
an	indefinite article	close	
bank		onto	
to drink		the	definite article
was carried		safely	
drowning		shortly afterwards	
and		stung	
it		pain	

The Peacock and the Crane

Feeling proud as it spread its gorgeous tail feathers, a peacock teased a crane that passed by. He laughed at the other bird because of the dull colour of its feathers. The peacock said rudely, "I am dressed like a king, in gold and purple and all the colours of the rainbow, while you have not a bit of colour on your wings."

"True," replied the crane, "but I can soar to the edge of space and lift up my voice to the stars, while you walk below like a cock among the birds of the dunghill."

B This time, find examples of the different word classes in the text to complete the table. One has been done for you.

Example from text	Word class	Example from text	Word class
	countable noun		adverb
	coordinating conjunction		adverbial
	uncountable noun		present participle
	subordinate conjunction	teased	past tense verb
	abstract noun		preposition
	pronoun		modal verb

C Write your own sentences using the two word classes in brackets.

Example: (proper noun/adjective) Prague is my favourite city.

(abstract noun/pronoun) _____

(subordinate conjunction/preposition) _____

_____

(present participle/adverb) _____

_____

Shades of meaning

The Boy Who Cried Wolf

There was once a shepherd boy who sat in the **hot** heat of the morning sun on the hillside, watching over the village sheep.

He was bored. To amuse himself, he suddenly had an idea. He took a deep breath and **shouted**: "Wolf! Wolf! The wolf is chasing the sheep!"

The villagers immediately came **running** up the hill to help the boy chase the wolf away. When they saw there was no wolf, they were **angry**. "Don't cry 'wolf' if there is no wolf," said the villagers. They went back down the hill, **complaining** as they walked.

Later that morning, the boy was still bored. Although he knew it was wrong, he **shouted** again: "Wolf! Wolf! The wolf is chasing the sheep!"

To his satisfaction, the boy watched the villagers run up the hill again to help him chase the wolf away.

When the villagers realised there was no wolf a second time, they were really **angry** and went back down the hill, **complaining** even more.

That afternoon, the shepherd boy saw a real wolf creeping up to the sheep. **Scared**, he jumped to his feet and screamed: "Wolf! Wolf!"

But the villagers thought he was fooling around and no one came to help him. The boy sat down and **cried** as there was nothing he could do to save the sheep.

 1 Replace the words in bold with more powerful words with the same meaning from the box below to make the text more interesting.

> furious wailed sweltering bellowed petrified yelled racing outraged
> grumbling sobbed scorching wept moaning fuming bawled tearing
> protesting whining terrified terror-stricken sprinting spooked blazing
> dashing sizzling hollered enraged roared

2 Put the words into six **synonym** sets. *Example:* sweltering, scorching, sizzling, blazing

_____

_____

_____

_____

_____

_____

Using adjectives

Putting adjectives into the right order

Adjectives should be used in a specific order. For example, size comes before colour so you would say 'a big red balloon'. This is the order adjectives should come in:

1 personal opinion   2 size   3 shape   4 colour

a   beautiful   big   round   red   balloon

A   **Put the adjectives in brackets in the correct order to describe the noun.**

   1   a tree (golden, stunning, tall) _____

   2   a cat (ginger, smelly, big) _____

   3   a skyscraper (wonderful, tall,) _____

   4   a plate (little, round) _____

   5   a hat (blue, comfortable, large) _____

B   **Write two or three adjectives to describe the following nouns.**
   (Note: you wouldn't usually use more than three adjectives to describe
   a noun.)

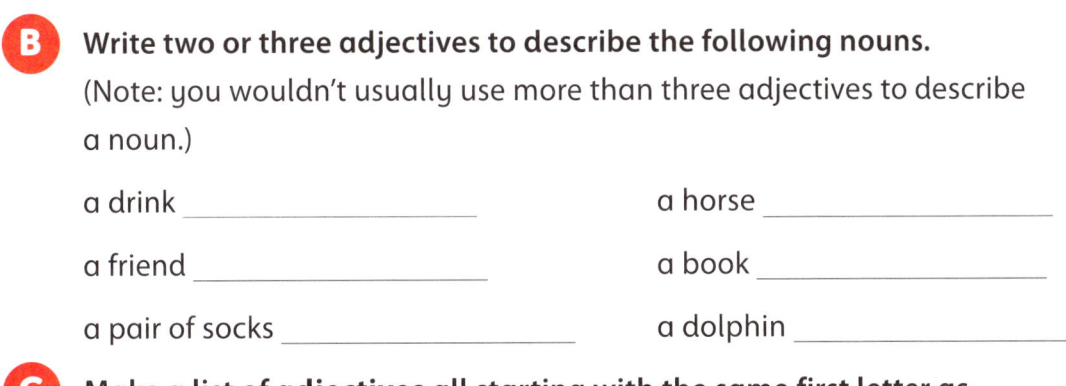

   a drink _____   a horse _____

   a friend _____   a book _____

   a pair of socks _____   a dolphin _____

C   **Make a list of adjectives all starting with the same first letter as
   someone's name. Don't worry about the order.**

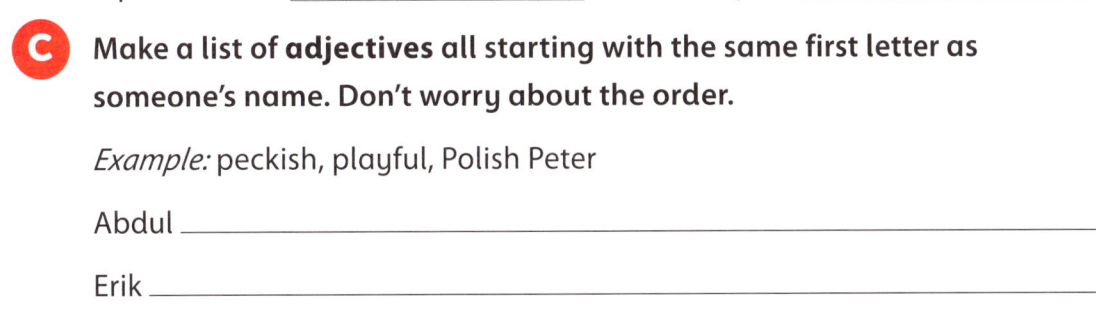

   Example: peckish, playful, Polish Peter

   Abdul _____

   Erik _____

   Mary _____

   Lee _____

   Siti _____

   Or a name of your own choice.

_____

Getting the spelling right

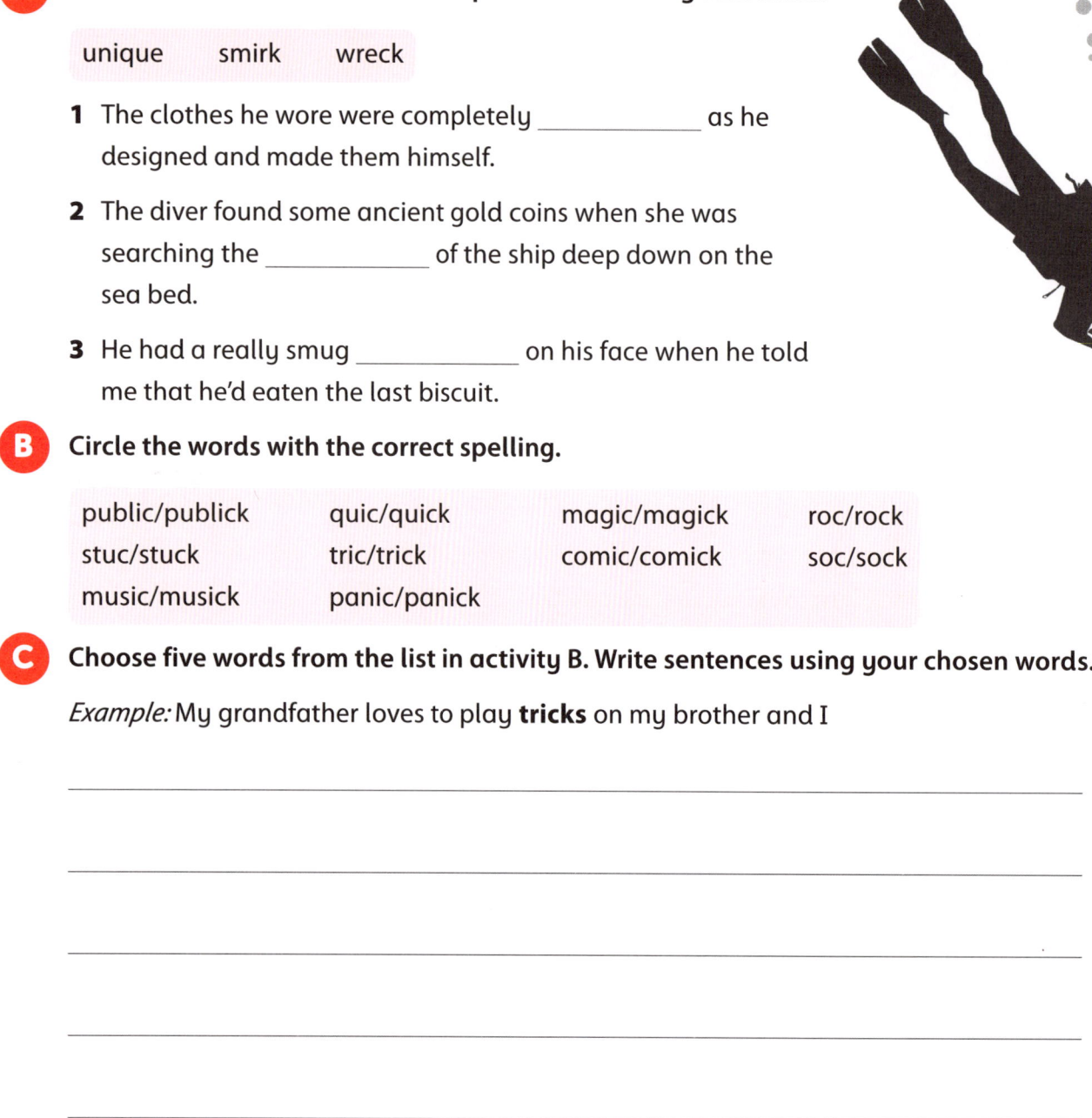

A Choose a word from below to complete the following sentences.

| unique | smirk | wreck |

1 The clothes he wore were completely _____ as he designed and made them himself.

2 The diver found some ancient gold coins when she was searching the _____ of the ship deep down on the sea bed.

3 He had a really smug _____ on his face when he told me that he'd eaten the last biscuit.

B Circle the words with the correct spelling.

public/publick	quic/quick	magic/magick	roc/rock
stuc/stuck	tric/trick	comic/comick	soc/sock
music/musick	panic/panick		

C Choose five words from the list in activity B. Write sentences using your chosen words.

Example: My grandfather loves to play **tricks** on my brother and I

_____

_____

_____

_____

_____

Check my learning

Unit 4 Traditional tales and fables

Name _____

Date _____

☺ I understand and I can do this well.

😐 I understand, but I am not confident.

☹ I don't understand and this is difficult.

Learning objective	☺	😐	☹
Reading skills			
I can use different types of words like adjectives and adverbs correctly.			
I can recognise the features of traditional and folk tales.			
I can answer questions based on information in a text.			
I can work out the meaning of words from context.			
I can find the meaning of phrasal verbs.			
I can choose an appropriate moral for a story.			
Writing skills			
I can recognise different word classes and use them correctly in my own writing.			
I can recognise that words have shades of meaning and use more powerful words to make my writing more interesting.			
I can use appropriate adjectives and adverbs in my writing.			

I would like more help with _____

_____

_____

5 School days

Persuasive text

Writing to convince

A Read these advertising slogans (1–6) and match them to the product they are selling (a–f).

1 Snuggle up in warm, handmade luxury.
2 Stay connected
3 Freshly squeezed glaciers
4 Doesn't your dog deserve it?
5 The ultimate driving experience
6 Fun, anyone?

a dog food
b bottled water
c a car
d a mobile phone
e a games console
f a jumper

B Read the advertisment below for *Manic Mania*, a computer game, then complete the text by filling the gaps with one of these **adverbs** or **adjectives**.

| brilliant | extreme | intense | amazingly | sensational |
| grippingly | fabulous | electrifying | thrilling | awesome |

Get ready for the most _____ adventure of your life!
Based on the classic Manic game, *Manic Mania*, the most _____
fast ride so far races onto your screen.

Six new _____ characters race at _____ speed. With
such _____ graphics and _____ new customised
supercars, this will be the most _____, the most
_____, the most _____ ride you'll
ever want to experience. Have you got what it takes?
Then prepare to be blown away!

A **1** Match the words from the advertsment in activity B with their definitions.

Circle the two words which are **synonyms**.

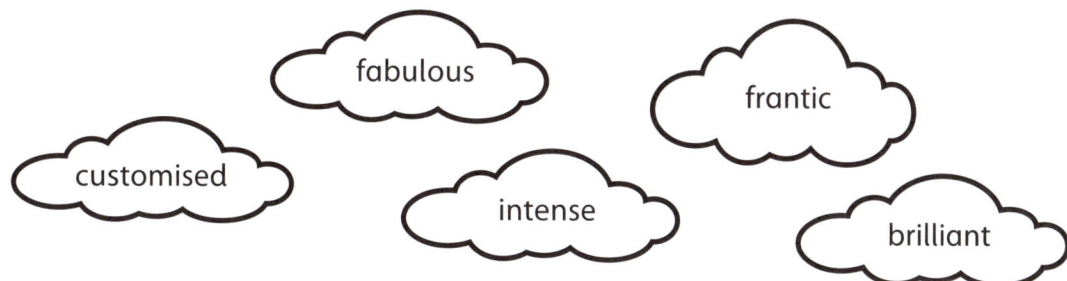

a _____ extremely good

b _____ built to individual or personal preference

c _____ desperate or wild with excitement or fear

d _____ serious, extreme

e _____ very impressive

2 Write your own advertising slogans for:

- your favourite snack

- your favourite meal

- your best friend

- your brother/sister

- your bedroom.

_____

_____

_____

_____

_____

_____

_____

Using the right linking word

Choose the right word

A **Put the correct linking word into the gaps below.**

consequently   especially   finally   as soon as
despite   however   because   next

Agnes was sitting in her seat waiting for the circus to begin. _____ , the curtain went up and there was the ringmaster. _____ being quite far back, Agnes could see perfectly. _____ the ringmaster had said "Hello", the clowns burst onto the stage. One had a large bucket of water which he was throwing everywhere. _____ , the people in the front row were getting rather wet. _____ , everybody was laughing _____ they didn't mind a bit of water. _____ came the acrobats. Agnes loved them, _____ the beautiful lady on the white horse.

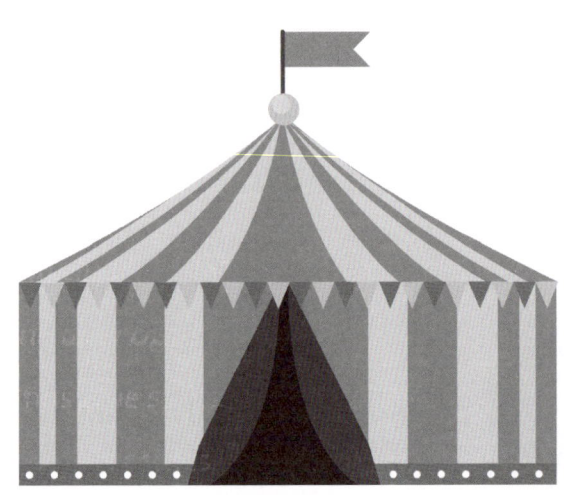

B **1 Put the linking words below into the correct category.**

unlike   after   also   as soon as   but   next
as well as   like   second   such as   finally   furthermore
too   in the same way   first   yet   so   on the other hand
because   thirdly   while

Adding _____

Comparing _____

Contrasting _____

Sequencing _____

Showing _____

Cause and effect _____

2 Write sentences using four of the linking words.

_____

_____

_____

_____

_____

_____

_____

_____

C Choose the correct linking word to complete the sentence.

1 My friends and I decided to walk to the swimming pool, _____ (consequently/unlike/whereas) my brother waited for Mum to give him a lift.

2 _____ (in particular/like/in the same way) me, my brother has to get up early to catch the bus for school.

3 My dad cooked the dinner _____ (as soon as/for example/ next) he got back from work.

4 I don't like eating breakfast in the morning _____ (because/ although/therefore) it makes me feel ill.

5 I like to stay inside and read, _____ (unlike/especially/unless) when it is wet and cold outside.

6 I love apples _____ (as well as/moreover/except) bananas.

7 I love all fruit, _____ (as long as/except/too) bananas.

8 Big dogs, _____ (therefore/such as/despite) mine, need a lot of exercise every day.

Relative clauses

Relative clauses are used to add information about nouns. They are introduced by relative pronouns.

- **who** refers to people

- **which** refers to animals, places or things

- **that** can refer to a person, place or thing

A Add the correct relative pronoun to the following sentences. In some sentences, there is more than one correct answer.

1 Babka lives in Zilina, _____ is a town in Slovakia.

2 That's the girl _____ lives near the park.

3 Demetri likes the book _____ is about African animals.

4 Mum is cross with the person _____ keeps leaving the door open.

5 She has lots of shirts but doesn't like the one _____ has blue spots.

B Sometimes a relative clause can be an embedded clause when it comes in the middle of a sentence. Add the correct relative pronoun to the following embedded clauses.

1 My grandad, _____ is 87, swims in the sea every day.

2 The old red house, _____ has been empty for years, is a bit spooky.

3 His most famous song, _____ was a great success, was written in half an hour.

C Complete these sentences.

1 They are going to move to Kuala Lumpur, which _____
_____

2 On the way to school, we always see a _____
who _____

3 My wealthy uncle has a _____ which _____
_____

4 I have been learning English, _____ ,
since I started school.

5 The Indian tiger, _____ ,
is a magnificent beast.

For or against?

When we write an argument, we have to:

- decide whether we are **for** or **against** an idea

- present **opinions** clearly and in a **logical order**

- give **evidence** or tell a true story to support our point of view

- **persuade** the reader to accept our view.

1 Read these two letters to a newspaper. Which letter is for allowing animals to perform in a circus? Which letter is against?

Letter 1

I am writing to express my outrage that animals were performing at the circus in West Park. In my view, animals should not be allowed to perform in circuses.

Wild animals like elephants, monkeys and tigers should live in their natural habitat, which is the jungle. For example, monkeys would be much happier swinging through the trees rather than swinging from the top of a circus tent. In my opinion, we should set circus animals free.

Secondly, the trainers are mistreating the animals to make them do tricks. I know this because the elephant's rider was hitting it with a stick. In addition, the Animal Protection Society claims that three-quarters of circus animals are cruelly treated.

In conclusion, if any readers are thinking of buying tickets for the circus next week, I urge them to think again. If you want to see wild animals, go to a wildlife park, not to a circus.

Yours faithfully,

J Gomez

In my view, circus animals are unhappy.

2 Use these phrases from Letter 1 to complete Letter 2.

I am writing to express my	For example	In my opinion
In addition	In conclusion	Yours faithfully

Letter 2

_____ support for allowing animals to perform in circuses.

_____, animals love to please people and enjoy doing tricks.

Many of these animals were not born in the jungle but reared by loving trainers.

They would not know how to survive in the jungle – they would probably get eaten by other animals.

_____, some animals would not be alive if they were not in the circus.

_____, tigers are endangered because their jungle habitats are being cut down. _____, there is no harm in keeping circus animals as long as they are looked after properly.

_____

Kiran Grover

B **Should children be film stars? Below is a list of arguments for (F) and against (A). Circle 'F' or 'A' to show which phrases are for and which are against.**

1 Child stars grow up too fast. F / A

2 Child stars can earn a lot of money. F / A

3 They miss school, so they get poor exam results. F / A

4 They often become stars in later life. F / A

5 They can become big-headed and greedy. F / A

6 They meet a lot of interesting people. F / A

C **Write a letter to a newspaper arguing for or against children becoming film stars.**

_____

_____

_____

_____

Check my learning

Unit 5 School days

Name _____

Date _____

☺ I understand and I can do this well.

😐 I understand, but I am not confident.

☹ I don't understand and this is difficult.

Learning objective	☺	😐	☹
Reading skills			
I can understand how the author influences a reader by using language of persuasion.			
I can recognise the appropriate adverb or adjective to join ideas.			
I can identify relative clauses.			
Writing skills			
I can write advertising slogans in an appropriate style.			
I can use linking words to structure my work.			
I can use a wide range of linking words.			
I can use the style of persuasive writing as a model for my own writing.			

I would like more help with _____

_____

_____

_____

6 Let's celebrate!

Read the poem.

It's Festival Time

A festival! A festival!

A friendly, family festival.

The time of year that's best of all.

A festival! A festival!

When food is most _____,

And games are all _____,

And presents are _____.

A festival! A festival!

A friendly, _____ festival.

A time of year that's _____.

A festival! A festival!

Sing songs and sound _____.

Religions east and west have all

got days they call a festival.

A festival, a festival!

A friendly, family festival.

The time of year that's best of all.

A festival! A festival!

A **1** Complete the poem by adding one of the words/phrases below. Make sure what you write makes sense. Use a dictionary to look up any words you don't know.

> best of all   requestable   celestial
> family   contestable   digestible

2 What activities does the poem describe people doing in festivals?

_____

_____

3 'A friendly, family festival'

What do you call the figurative technique that has been used in this sentence?

_____

B **1** Write another verse to the poem by filling in the gaps with your own ideas. You can use the words below to help you. You might want to make up some words.

> changeable beautiful carnival laughable edible extendable
> flexible delectable plentiful spectacle colourful

A festival! A festival!

When sweets are _____ ,

And we all make a _____ ,

And bedtime is _____ .

2 Write one more verse, using the verse above as your model.

_____

_____

_____

_____

_____

Read your new poem to the class.

Spellings

A **Choose the correct spelling to complete the sentences.**

1 You borrow books from a _____ .

library

libary

libry

2 Not all snake bites are _____ .

posernous

poisonous

poisernous

3 It was the most _____ film I've ever seen.

frighterning

frightning

frightening

4 Can you _____ your dirty clothes so I can wash them?

seperate

separate

seperait

5 The comments she made were very _____ .

interesting

intresting

inturesting

B **Correct the spelling mistakes in the following paragraph.**

The calinder showd it wos 6th June and it wos necessery for me to rember that it wood be my brofers berthday in free days' thyme. He wood be misrable if I didn't get him a precent so I desparately fought whot I coud get him wifout spending to much monee and came up wiv a marvollos idear – a book culled *The Tempest* by William Shakespeer.

C Complete the crossword.

Down

1 Another word for occurred.

2 This is how tall something is.

3 The opposite of forget.

4 When you have a disagreement.

5 A homophone of 'court'.

6 When something is needed, it is …

Across

4 The place you live in or stay at.

7 Another word for the start of something e.g. a story.

8 When you feel awkward, ashamed or self-conscious.

9 The noun of strong.

Difficult words and homophones

Spelling correctly

A Choose the correct **homophone** to complete the sentences.

accept/except	desert/dessert	course/cause
saw/sore	mail/male	bald/bold	ate/eight

1 I'm expecting a letter. Has the _____ been delivered yet?

2 I can't go to school today because I have a cold and my throat
is _____.

3 He hasn't got a single hair on his head. He is completely
_____.

4 Hannah could not _____ Sanketh's invitation as she was
already busy that day.

5 "Who _____ all my sweets?" cried my _____
year old brother.

6 "You can't have _____ unless you finish your main
_____ first," said Mum.

B Some of the following words have been mis-spelled. Write the correct
spelling next to any words that you think have the wrong spelling.

definite _____   disapoint _____

embarress _____   nesessary _____

seperate _____   strenth _____

beatiful _____   dissapear _____

beggining _____   believe _____

C Rearrange the jumbled up letters below to create words which
are often spelt incorrectly. You have been given the first letter
of each word.

umreantg argument_____   pomceellty c_____

ibsssune b_____   llnifay f_____

igmocn c_____   mariilaf f_____

Poetic devices

 A Look at the following sentences and identify which poetic technique is used. Some techniques have been used more than once and some sentences use more than one technique.

metaphor	simile	hyperbole	personification
onomatopoeia	rhyme	repetition	alliteration

1 A ton of worry was lifted from her shoulders. _____

2 It's cool, it's fun and it's all mine. _____

3 She slipped into a silent slumber. _____

4 The wild wind whooshed as the rain tip-tap-splatted on the window.

_____

5 She's like a cat dozing in the sun. _____

6 The moon smiled timidly, then disappeared behind a cloud.

_____

7 His eyes are oceans. _____

8 The cake is as sweet as honey, made by buzzing bees as big as battleships. _____

9 The star sailed away on a silver mist. _____

10 The cat sat on her cosy, warm mat. _____

B Complete these sentences using poetic devices.

1 The sun _____.

2 _____ as a deer.

3 His head was spinning with _____.

4 My teacher is _____.

5 Swish, swoosh went _____.

6 My favourite _____.

7 _____ as a raging bull.

8 I've told you a million times _____.

_____

C **1** Think of your favourite celebration and write some sentences using each of the poetic devices in activity A to describe it. (You could use some techniques more than once in a sentence.)

Examples: The fireworks go *whoosh, fizz, bang, pop*.

The mithai are as sweet as sticky syrup.

_____

_____

_____

_____

_____

_____

_____

_____

_____

_____

2 Use the lines you think work best to make a poem describing your favourite festival.

_____

_____

_____

_____

_____

Check my learning

Unit 6 Let's celebrate!

Name _____

Date _____

😊 I understand and I can do this well.

😐 I understand, but I am not confident.

☹️ I don't understand and this is difficult.

Learning objective	😊	😐	☹️
Reading skills			
I can recognise and understand different poetic devices.			
I can read and interpret poems.			
I can recognise how poets play with words and sounds.			
Writing skills			
I can spell words with unstressed vowels.			
I can spell different words correctly, including homophones.			
I can use a poem as a model for my own writing.			
I can use figurative language in my own writing.			

I would like more help with _____

_____

_____

7 Spies and mystery

Using the mystery genre in writing

Read this extract from *Stormbreaker* by Anthony Horowitz.

Alex is in a metal scrapyard where they crush cars into small lumps of metal to reuse. He has taken his dead uncle's car there to be crushed but then he sees two men with guns coming in his direction.

And then something hit the car with such force that Alex cried out, his whole body caught in a <u>massive</u> (_____) shock wave that <u>tore</u> (_____) him away from the steering-wheel and threw him helplessly into the back. At the same time, the roof <u>buckled</u> (_____) and three huge metal fingers tore through the skin of the car like a fork through an eggshell, trailing dust and sunlight. One of the fingers <u>grazed</u> (_____) the side of his head – any closer and it would have <u>cracked</u> (_____) his skull. Alex yelled as blood <u>trickled</u> (_____) over his eye. He tried to move, then was <u>jerked</u> (_____) back a second time as the car was <u>yanked</u> (_____) off the ground and <u>tilted</u> (_____) high in the air.

He couldn't see. He couldn't move. But his stomach <u>lurched</u> (_____) as the car swung in an arc, the metal <u>grinding</u> (_____) and the light <u>spinning</u> (_____). He had been picked up by the crane. It was going to put the car inside the crusher. With him inside.

A Replace each of the underlined words in the extract with a synonym listed below.

Make sure that the new word has the same meaning as the word it replaces and fits in the context of the sentence.

broken	bent	ripped	tipped	grating	huge
scraped	dripped	jumped	wrenched	pulled	whirling

B **Answer the following questions using words and phrases from the extract.**

1 What threw Alex to the back of the car the first time? _____

_____

2 Was it difficult for the machine to break through the metal of the car?
Use words from the passage to explain your answer.

_____

_____

3 Why was Alex thrown to the back of the car for a second time?

_____

4 What made Alex's stomach uneasy?

_____

5 Why did Alex need to leave the car as quickly as possible?

_____

C **Look at the extract again.**

1 Write examples of short sentences from the extract. What effect do they have?
Why does the writer use short sentences sometimes?

_____

_____

_____

2 Write examples of powerful, descriptive verbs and adverbs used in the text.

_____

3 Find an example of a simile in the text. What meaning does it express?
Why did the writer use it?

_____

_____

_____

4 Find an example of a metaphor in the text. What meaning does it express?
Why did the writer use it?

_____

_____

_____

Idioms

 A How good is your knowledge of idioms? Take the idiom quiz and see!

1 When something is on your bucket list it is something:

    a you really dislike

    b you want to do

    c you always carry

2 If you do something by the skin of your teeth:

    a you only just manage to do it

    b you do it but very reluctantly

    c you do it without effort

3 If something happens once in a blue moon:

    a it never happens

    b it happens regularly

    c it happens very occasionally

4 If something is a piece of cake it is:

    a soft

    b easy

    c tempting

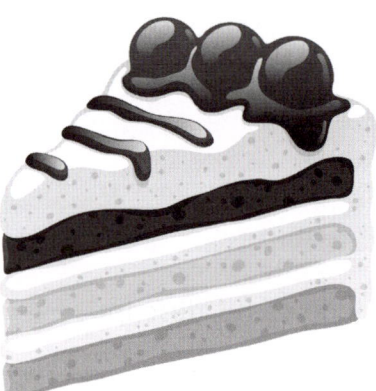

5 If you hit the sack you:

    a do your work

    b disappear for a while

    c go to bed

6 If you have bitten off more than you can chew you have:

    a taken on a task that's too big

    b put more on your plate than you can eat

    c made yourself seem cleverer than you are

7 If you see eye to eye with someone you are:

    a working with them closely

    b giving them an admiring look

    c in agreement with them

8 If you go that extra mile you:

    a are absolutely exhausted

    b make a special effort

    c walk further than anyone else

9 If you spill the beans you:

    a make a mess

    b give a secret away

    c are a messy eater

10 If you're told to sit tight, you should:

    a wait patiently

    b be ready to move quickly

    c not change your mind

Check your answers at the bottom of the page.

> If you got 7–10 correct answers, you're an idiom expert!
>
> If you got 4–6 correct answers, you've got good idiom knowledge.
>
> If you got 0–3 correct answers, maybe you should do some research on idioms.

B **Do you know what any of the following idioms mean?**

- rings a bell _____
- no-brainer _____
- face the music _____
- pull yourself together _____
- take with a pinch of salt _____

7 = c, 8 = b, 9 = b, 10 = a

1 = b, 2 = a, 3 = c, 4 = b, 5 = c, 6 = a,

Active and passive

A In Standard English, it is more common to use the active voice because the passive voice makes the information longer and it can seem awkward. Sometimes, though, writers choose to use the passive voice for one of the reasons below. Match the reasons below. The first one has been done for you.

to make the tone	is not known
because the subject	more exciting
to take the emphasis away from the subject because	more formal
to make a narrative	it is not as important as the object

B Say whether the following sentences are active ('A'), passive ('P') or both ('B'). Circle the correct letters to give your answer. Then rewrite active sentences as passive and passive sentences as active in the space below.

1 A 500-year-old diamond necklace was found in an old piano. **A / P / B**

_____

2 In the final moment, Foden scored the winning goal for Manchester City! **A / P / B**

_____

3 The birthday cake has been eaten up by somebody. **A / P / B**

_____

4 Coats must be hung on the pegs provided. **A / P / B**

_____

5 The valuable vase was stolen by thieves in broad daylight. **A / P / B**

_____

6 Noodles should be eaten with chopsticks. **A / P / B**

_____

7 Our maths teacher gave us loads of homework. **A / P / B**

_____

8 I put the apple, which had been half eaten, in the bin. **A / P / B**

_____

9 We saw a car that was being driven very fast by its owner. **A / P / B**

_____

10 A girl aged five was saved by a zookeeper when she fell into the tiger enclosure. **A / P / B**

_____

C **1** Finish these sentences with a passive verb.

Example: A priceless painting was found in the cellar of a deserted, old house.

a A box of valuable jewels _____

b A group of school children _____

c The tiger _____

d Apples _____

e A lot of food _____

2 Make up three intriguing newspaper headings in the passive form.
Example: Parrot is seized after egging others on.

_____

_____

_____

Adverbials of time

A Find the following words hidden in the square.

after a while	finally	since
afterwards	in the end	soon
at once	later on	straightaway
at this moment	meanwhile	until then
before that	next time	whenever
next	previously	when

b	e	f	o	r	e	t	h	a	t	n	i	o	p	s	i	h	t	t	a
f	i	n	a	l	l	y	i	n	t	h	e	e	n	d	h	e	r	e	t
a	f	t	e	r	a	w	h	i	l	e	m	m	a	x	q	p	u	j	t
f	i	w	h	e	n	h	a	w	s	w	h	e	n	e	v	e	r	a	h
t	r	v	b	t	o	i	l	q	t	r	a	m	o	t	s	w	e	m	i
e	s	o	o	n	w	l	e	y	l	a	t	e	r	o	n	v	u	e	s
r	t	m	e	a	n	e	x	t	y	b	o	n	d	t	h	e	n	s	m
w	m	e	a	n	w	h	i	l	e	t	e	c	n	i	s	u	t	w	o
a	t	o	n	c	e	n	e	x	t	t	i	m	e	r	i	d	e	r	m
r	p	r	e	c	i	o	u	s	y	l	s	u	o	i	v	e	r	p	e
d	s	f	n	e	h	t	l	i	t	n	u	t	c	n	i	s	p	o	n
s	o	n	a	n	o	t	h	e	r	o	c	c	a	s	i	o	n	z	t
s	y	a	w	a	t	h	g	i	a	r	t	s	·	a	r	i	o	p	q	u

B Write five sentences using an adverbial of time.

_____

_____

_____

_____

_____

Check my learning

Unit 7 Spies and mystery

Name _____

Date _____

☺ I understand and I can do this well.

😐 I understand, but I am not confident.

☹ I don't understand and this is difficult.

Learning objective	☺	😐	☹
Reading skills			
I can identify synonyms which could be replaced in a text.			
I can answer questions based on information in a text.			
I can analyse how a writer builds up tension.			
I can comment on a writer's use of English.			
I can understand the meaning of idioms.			
I can recognise why passive forms are used.			
Writing skills			
I can write sentences in the active and passive form.			
I can write sentences which include an adverbial of time.			

I would like more help with _____

_____

_____

_____

 # Conserving our precious planet

The best trip ever!

"We'll go to Italy to celebrate the end of your exams, Katarina," my father announced. "We will have a road trip and drive across Europe to get there." I was so excited!

That was six months ago. A month before we were due to go, my uncle announced that his wedding would be right in the middle of our planned trip. No matter. My father decided to bring the trip forward. My brothers and parents would drive across Europe to Italy: a journey that would take three days.

I would stay with my cousins for a few days, take my final exam, then fly out to Verona: a journey that would take two and a half hours. My family would arrive a few hours earlier, unpack our stuff and settle into our apartment overlooking Lake Garda. Then my father would collect me from the airport.

Everything had gone smoothly – I had been so proud of myself because it was my first flight alone. But at Verona airport, I was beginning to panic. I had been waiting one and a quarter hours and there was no sign of my father. I had no Euros, spoke no Italian and had no idea which town we were staying in, let alone the name of the apartment. It was dusk. A hot, summer storm rumbled overhead and big fat raindrops started to fall. And that's when I saw my brother's cheeky face walking quickly towards me – I have never been so pleased to see him in my life!

A **1** What are the family celebrating? _____

2 Why do they have to change their plans? _____

3 Why can't Katarina go with the rest of her family? _____

4 Why is Katarina proud of herself? _____

5 What changed her mood?_____

6 Why was Katarina happy at the end of the passage? _____

_____

B Write a paragraph from Katarina's point of view to say what happens next.

_____

_____

_____

_____

Working on a passage

Commas

A Read the passage below and add commas where necessary.

Recently a memorial was put up in the centre of my city in honour of a man known as Snowy who worked relentlessly to raise money for animal charities. I remember Snowy very well.

Always dressed in colourful clothes and a brightly coloured top hat Snowy was a gentle caring man who loved and was loved by all the local children. They would look at him in awe as he played all his musical instruments which included cymbals drums an accordion a harmonica and a recorder. They were all somehow connected so he could play them all at once!

Writing instructions

B Write the instructions for how to get from the writer's house (labelled 'My house') to Snowy's memorial. Instead of numbering the instructions, use an adverbial of time such as first, then, after that, finally.

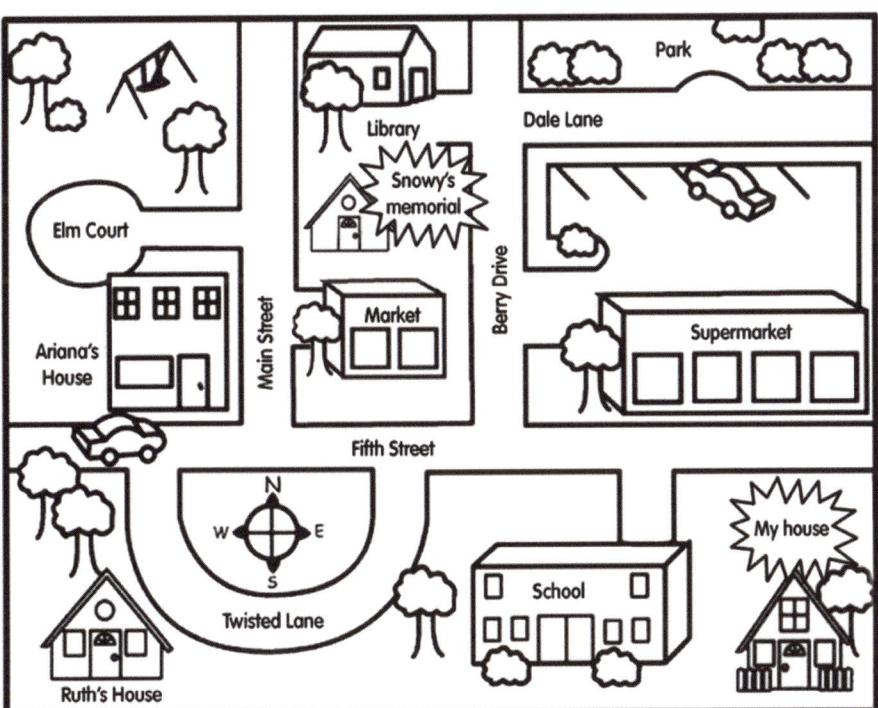

_____

_____

_____

Writing instructions

A Write the instructions for drawing a top hat like Snowy's. Write one instruction for each illustration. Add adverbials of time to show the order and adverbs to tell the reader how to do something (*for example*: carefully, gently).

Linking the heading and paragraphs in non-fiction text

 A Read this information extract. Then write four appropriate subheadings for the extract in the spaces provided.

Pangolins: The World's Most Trafficked Mammals

_____

Pangolins are insect-eating mammals that are covered in tough, overlapping scales. There are eight pangolin species living across Asia and Africa.

_____

More than 1 million pangolins have been **trafficked** in the last decade. Their scales are used in traditional Asian medicines and their meat is considered a luxury food throughout Asia.

_____

All eight species of pangolins are now threatened with extinction. Pangolins are a protected species and it's illegal to sell or buy them, but much more work needs to be done! We are working with rangers and wildlife authorities in the places where pangolins are hunted and providing them with resources to stop the hunters.

_____

One major problem is that most people don't even know that pangolins exist. People around the world need to be educated about pangolins and the crisis they are in. Your donations will support the most effective pangolin conservation projects in Africa and Asia.

Pangolins are the most trafficked wild mammals in the world. But it is not too late to save them from extinction!

B Summarise the main points in the third paragraph, using as few words as possible.

1 _____

_____

Paragraphs and subheadings

A Complete this text about avalanches by adding the sentences below to the correct paragraphs.

> An avalanche can <u>occur</u> on any slope at any time if the conditions are right, but most avalanches occur after heavy snowfall.
>
> Many avalanches are just small slides of powdery snow moving down a slope as a formless mass.

Avalanches

What is an avalanche?

An avalanche is the sudden <u>forceful</u> flow of snow down a hill or mountainside.

_____

_____

Larger <u>scale</u> avalanches happen when massive <u>slabs</u> of snow break loose from a mountain and travel down the slope at speeds of up to 125 kilometres per hour in five seconds.

What causes an avalanche?

_____

_____ This means that avalanches usually happen between December and April.

What _____

One of the worst effects of an avalanche is that it can clear a whole area of trees, which then becomes an area <u>more prone to</u> avalanches in following years.

B Look at the subheadings for paragraphs 1 and 2. Write an appropriate subheading for paragraph 3.

C **Using the information in the extract, answer these questions.**

1 At what time of year is an avalanche most likely to happen?

_____

2 How fast can an avalanche travel?

_____

3 What is the most common cause of an avalanche?

_____

4 Do avalanches always occur after heavy snowfall? How do you know?

_____

5 What effect do some avalanches have on the environment?

_____

D **1** Why is an area without trees more likely to have an avalanche than an area with trees?

_____

_____

2 Is this text all facts, mainly facts or a mixture of facts and opinions?

_____

_____

3 Replace the underlined words in the extract with a **synonym** from the box below.

| happen | more likely to have | blocks | sized | powerful |

Quantifiers

A Complete the sentences below using one of the **quantifiers** from the box. Use a different one in each gap.

> box   enough   a couple   any   loads   some   plenty of

"I'm going to buy _____ sugar to make a cake."

"We don't need _____ sugar because we have _____ it left."

"Are you sure we have _____ sugar to make a cake?"

"I'm telling you, we have _____ !"

"OK. What about eggs?"

"We've got _____ . Is that enough?"

"No, I need three."

"Alright, go to the shop and buy a _____ of eggs."

B Write your own sentences using the word in brackets

1 (some) _____

2 (any) _____

3 (enough) _____

4 (plenty of) _____

5 (a few) _____

6 (many) _____

C Can you think of quantifiers for the following food?

Examples: A bag of crisps   A tin of soup

A _____ of coke   A _____ of sweets

A _____ of potatoes   A _____ of eggs

A _____ of butter   A _____ of milk.

EGGS

MILK

BUTTER

SUGAR

Check my learning

Unit 8 Conserving our precious planet

Name _____

Date _____

☺ I understand and I can do this well.

😐 I understand, but I am not confident.

☹ I don't understand and this is difficult.

Learning objective	☺	😐	☹
Reading skills			
I can answer explicit questions using information from a text.			
I know what sort of language I should use in the different forms of non-chronological reports.			
I can discuss the language and grammatical features of different forms of non-chronological reports.			
Writing skills			
I can write clear instructions using adverbials of time.			
I can write sentences using quantifiers.			
I can write a paragraph to continue a recount.			

I would like more help with _____

_____

_____

_____

9 A treasure trove of poems

Punctuation

A Read this poem, then insert the missing punctuation for verses 7 and 8, such as apostrophes, speech marks and commas.

The ABC

1 'Twas midnight in the schoolroom
And every desk was shut,
When suddenly from the alphabet
Was heard a loud "Tut-Tut!"

2 Said A to B, "I dont like C;
His manners are a lack.
For all I ever see of C
Is a semi-circular back!"

3 "I disagree," said D to B,
"I've never found C so.
From where I stand, he seems to be
An uncompleted O."

4 C was vexed, "I'm much perplexed,
You criticise my shape.
I'm made like that, to help spell
Cat And Cow and Cool and Cape."

5 "He's right said E; said F,
"Whoopee!"
Said G, "'Ip, 'Ip, 'ooray!"
"You're dropping me," roared H to G.
"Don't do it please I pray!"

6 "Out of my way," LL said to K.
"I'll make poor I look ILL."
To stop this stunt, J stood in front,
And presto! ILL was JILL.

7 U know said V that W
Is twice the age of me.
For as a Roman V is five
I'm half as young as he.

8 X and Y yawned sleepily,
Look at the time! they said.
Lets all get off to beddy byes.
They did, then "Z-z-z."

Spike Milligan

B Answer these questions about the poem.

1 Why was A and D's understanding of C different? _____

_____

2 Why does V say he is half of W's age? _____

_____

3 Which letters of the alphabet were left out of the poem? _____

_____

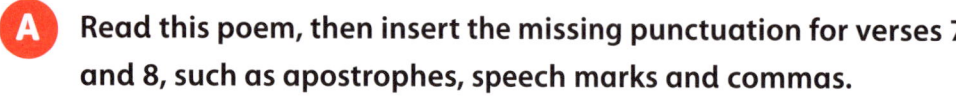

Creating pictures with words

Flood

The rain fell all night, beating on roofs
as dark and **hunched** as hills,
cascading uncontained into the street
in wind-curved waterfalls.

All night the rain fell, kept falling.
This morning, the street's a river:
cars **flounder** and sink, while buses
crawl **laden** as ocean liners,

raise bow-waves so **swollen** they break
booming across the pavement
where tossed at the tide's rising mark
seaweed tangles to litter;

and under the hedges and gates
fish **shoal** in the gleaming shallows,
and further out, through the channel
marked by wave-slapped traffic-lights,

dolphins leap lampposts, and whales
surge and sound in the deep roads.

Dave Calder

1 Which statement is true?

    a The poem is about life under the sea.

    b The poem describes somewhere after there has been a flood.

    c The poem is realistic.

2 Find a quote which shows what the poet says has happened to the cars.

_____

1 What does the poet compare the following objects to?

    a the roofs of the houses _____

    b the street _____

    c the buses _____

2 Find an example of each of these figurative language techniques in the first verse:

    a personification _____

    b simile _____

    c alliteration _____

Ups and downs

John Foster started to make up poems for his children to stop them from getting bored on long car journeys.

The Price of Fame

It's not easy being famous.

Last week I was a hero.
In injury time
my namesake scored the winner
5 with a glancing header.

Everyone ran round the playground
chanting my name.

Today I'm a villain.
Last night I missed an open goal.
10 Then, just after half time,
I was sent off for a professional foul.
We lost two-nil.

Everyone's blaming me and calling me names.

If it goes on like this,
15 I'm going to ask Sir for a transfer.

John Foster

Comprehension

 A **Answer these questions, using evidence from the poem.**

1 What are two consequences of the footballer being sent off?

2 What do you think the footballer means by 'I'm going to ask Sir for a transfer'?

3 The title of the poem is 'The Price of Fame'. What alternative title would also give the reader an idea of what the poem is about?

Compound words

A compound word is created when two or more words are combined to create a new word.

Example: door + mat = doormat

A Match a word (1–10) with another word (a–j) to make a new compound word.

1 grand		**a** book
2 some		**b** print
3 grass		**c** mother
4 tea		**d** end
5 house		**e** thing
6 note		**f** market
7 week		**g** hopper
8 snow		**h** work
9 super		**i** cup
10 finger		**j** flake

B Add the same word to each row to create new compound words.

Example: wheel**chair**   arm**chair**   push**chair**

a green _____   tree _____   light _____

b horse _____   dragon _____   fire _____

c sun _____   moon _____   fire _____

d flower _____   tea _____   jack _____

C Complete the following compound words by filling the gap with a part of the body. The first has been done for you.

Example: **ear**ache   **ear**phones   **ear**wax

a _____ brush   _____ paste   _____ pick

b _____ liner   _____ lash   _____ brow

c _____ ball   _____ print   _____ path

d _____ ache   _____ teacher   _____ line

Direct speech

A Below is an extract of a story from *Earth is Room Enough*, by Isaac Asimov. Using the sentences below to help you, explain the rules for how speech and dialogue should be punctuated and set out.

She said, "Where did you find it?"

"In my house." He pointed without looking because he was busy reading. "In the attic."

"What's it about?"

"School."

Margie was scornful. "School? What's there to write about school?

I hate school."

_____

_____

_____

_____

B Add in the missing punctuation and reporting clauses, such as 'he said' and 'she shouted'.

She read the book over his shoulder for a while, then said, "Anyway, they had a teacher

"Sure they had a teacher, but it wasn't a regular teacher. It was a man

A man? How could a man be a teacher"

"Well, he just told the boys and girls things and gave them homework and asked them questions

"A man isn't smart enough"

"Sure he is _____ My father knows as much as my teacher."

_____

"He cant _____ A man can't know as much as a teacher.

_____

Same sound, different spellings

A Underline the correct spelling of the following words.

1 pancake/pancack antick/antique trunck/trunk wrek/wreck pluck/pluke

2 swich/switch pouch/poutch mach/match stitch/stich thatch/thach

3 jiant/giant jiraffe/giraffe rige/ridge jeans/geans gaws/jaws

B Find the /ch/ and /j/ words in the word search.

j	e	l	l	y	d	o	d	g	e	b	e
i	t	c	h	u	r	c	h	a	i	r	m
s	w	i	t	c	h	i	t	c	h	i	e
t	w	i	t	c	h	u	t	c	h	d	r
g	i	n	g	e	r	b	e	a	d	g	g
e	a	c	h	a	t	c	h	o	t	e	e
o	r	c	h	a	r	d	i	t	c	s	n
g	i	r	a	f	f	e	g	e	m	c	c
r	j	u	n	k	r	i	d	g	e	r	y
a	g	e	n	t	l	e	j	o	g	a	w
p	u	n	c	h	g	e	r	m	s	t	a
h	o	g	l	i	t	c	h	r	o	c	g
y	j	a	g	u	a	r	a	t	c	h	e

C Do the following words make the /g/ sound or /j/ sound?

dodge gem gallop generate green budget began

/g/   /j/

_____   _____

_____   _____

_____   _____

_____   _____

Figures of speech

A Match the expressions (1–6) with their definitions (a–g).

1 bookworm

2 hot potato

3 mind reader

4 showstopper

5 black cloak

6 winter's blanket

a someone who knows what you're thinking

b snow

c a very popular performance

d something no one wants to deal with

e someone who reads a lot

f nightfall

B What creature is being described by these kennings? _____

treetop-squawker

loud-screecher

wing-flapper

colourful-splendour

jungle-treasure

C Write your own kenning for each of the following:

- sibling or best friend _____
- favourite game _____
- favourite food _____
- favourite music _____
- homework _____

Check my learning

Unit 9 A treasure trove of poems

Name _____

Date _____

☺ I understand and I can do this well.

😐 I understand, but I am not confident.

☹ I don't understand and this is difficult.

Learning objective	☺	😐	☹
Reading skills			
I have read poems by different well-known poets.			
I can answer questions about the ideas created in the poems.			
Writing skills			
I can spell and use compound words appropriately.			
I can use the correct spelling of the /ch/ and /j/ sounds.			
I can punctuate direct speech appropriately.			
I can write a kenning to describe someone or something.			

I would like more help with _____

_____

_____

_____

Pulling together

Oki was the finest young hunter of his people.
He could run like the wind and carry great loads
on his back. He could pull fish from the coldest
sea, and there was no one who could paddle a kayak
5 with such speed and skill.

Oki's older sister was called Anuat. She was restless
and adventurous. She liked running out along the shore,
hunting small birds and taking them home to eat.

"I want to see life!" she used to say to Oki. "It's so dull
10 here at home. I want to meet other people and go to
far-off places."

Oki's little sister was called Puja. She liked being at
home and helping her mother. They would cut up the
meat which Oki brought home, cook it and sew clothes
15 from the animal skins.

One winter's day, when the sea was quite frozen over,
Oki and the older sister, Anuat, went off over the ice
towards some distant islands.

"A fox! Look there! I'll catch him if I can!" shouted
20 Oki, and he raced away, as fast as a wind-blown bird.

The fox was fast, and the chase went on for many miles,
but at last Oki captured his prey. Pleased with himself, he
trudged back to the place where he had left his sister.

She wasn't there. He looked out over the frozen white
25 world and called as loudly as he could.

No one answered.

Then Oki saw marks in the snow. There were long
double stripes made by a sledge's runners, and between
them were the prints of reindeer hooves. All around, the
30 snow had been churned up, as if there had been a struggle.

"What can this mean?" he puzzled. "Has my sister been kidnapped? Why are there prints of reindeer hooves between the marks of the sledge runners?"

Baffled, Oki went home, hoping to find his sister
35 already there. But she hadn't returned. For days and days the family waited and hoped, but Anuat never came back.

Weeks passed, then months. No one talked about Anuat any more, but she was in Oki's mind all the time.

"I must find her. I must!" he said to himself.
40 Spring was coming now and the warm weather was melting the ice between the islands. Oki gazed out across the vast stretches of icy water. "If Anuat is still alive, she must be far away," he thought sadly.

But Oki was determined to find his sister. He thought
45 long and hard.

"When the sea freezes again, I will set out. But how can
I avoid hunger and exhaustion? If only I could move more
quickly over the ice."

Oki thought back to the reindeer prints between the
50 sledge marks. The seed of an idea planted itself in his mind.
Was it possible? There was only one way to find out …

The next time that Oki went hunting, he took with him a
sledge and some strong cords.

"Where are you going?" little Puja asked him. "What are
55 those cords for?"

"You'll see," said Oki, and off he ran, pulling the sledge
after him.

It was days before he came home. From inside their snow
house, Puja heard a strange noise. She ran outside to look
60 and screamed with fright.

"Father, Mother! Oki's come home, and he's
brought a monster with him!"

Her parents ran to look.

"This isn't a monster," laughed Oki. "It's a baby bear,
65 and I'm going to train him to pull my sledge."

Oki's father shook his head and smiled at his
son's folly. Oki didn't care. He made a harness
for the little white bear and taught him to run
ahead of the sledge, pulling it along behind
70 him. But the bear cub tired quickly and soon
lost interest. So off Oki went again.

A few days later, he came back. This time, unearthly howls brought Puja running out to look. She screamed even louder than before.

75   "Look at its teeth, and its great round eyes, and its horrid bushy tail!"

"It's nothing to be scared of!" scolded Oki. "What a baby you are! It's only a wolf cub. Now let's see what he can do."

80   Oki harnessed the bear cub and the wolf cub together, and tried to make them pull the sledge. But they fought each other, biting and scratching. They refused to make the sledge run at all.

Oki didn't give up. He made a special harness so that

85 the two young animals couldn't reach each other. He petted them, and gave them good food, and at last he made them run together. But the wolf ran fast, and the bear ran slowly. The sledge went round in circles!

Oki tried again. He caught another wolf cub, and this

90 time he trained all three to run together, with the bear in the middle. Now it was going well! Oki could ride on his sledge far and fast, and carry heavy loads, too.

* * *

Winter came again. The sea was once more frozen
into a vast sheet of ice. The sun hung low in the sky, and
95 night fell almost before it was day. Oki made a new sledge,
stronger and faster than his old one.

"I'm going to look for my sister," he told his parents. "I won't rest till
I've found her."

His father and mother were worried. "We've lost one of our children,"
100 they said. "How could we bear to lose another? Stay at home, son.
Forget your sister. She is lost to us forever."

But Oki was determined. "I have my animals now
to help me," he said. "We can cover miles and miles in
one day."

105 He set off, racing fast to the place where he had last seen
his sister, out on the ice that covered the sea.

Soon, the bear was tired and slowed the others down, so
Oki unhitched him and carried him on the sledge.

Now, with the wolves alone, the sledge shot forwards,
110 swishing across the ice faster than any person could
run. On and on went the wolves, while Oki cracked his
whip over their willing backs and shouted cries
of encouragement.

And so they crossed the sea, until at last they came to
115 the far shore where the ground was rough and uneven.
It was impossible to run the sledge over it.

Oki hitched his sledge to an iceberg and gave each of his
animals a big chunk of meat to eat. Then on he went on
foot, alone. He was tired and hungry but he wouldn't
120 turn back.

"I'll find you, Anuat. I'll find you!" he muttered to
himself through the freezing wind that ruffled the fur
edging to his hood.

At last, he came to a settlement of igloos. A woman
125 came out at his call. It was Anuat herself, and in her
arms was a baby, all muffled up in fur.

"Oki!" she cried, her face lighting up with delight.
"How did you get here? How did you find me?"

He followed her into her igloo, and the brother and

135 sister talked long into the night.

"That day," Anuat said, "when you ran off after the fox, some strangers came past. They snatched me up and carried me away on their sledge. It was pulled by a reindeer, so we were soon far beyond anywhere I had

140 been before. I fought and struggled, but they wouldn't let me go.

"Eventually we reached this land and I was forced to stay. But then I met a good kind man here. We fell in love and married. Look, we have a baby now! There was only

145 one thing that was making me unhappy, and that was the thought of my family, worried and wondering where I was.

"Now you have come all this way to find me! But how did you do it, Oki? How did you come so far across the sea ice, on your own?"

150 "I'll show you in the morning, if you'll come down to the edge of the sea ice with me," said Oki, yawning. "But now, dear sister, I want something to eat. In fact, I want a feast! So let me see what's in that pot bubbling so hard on the fire. I could eat a whole seal all by myself!"

150 And from that day to this, people have used the descendants of wolves to pull their sledges across the frozen Arctic landscapes.

Elizabeth Laird

Glossary

armour *noun* metal clothing to protect soldiers

banishing *verb* punishing someone by sending them away and ordering them not to return

banquet *noun* a large formal dinner

beckoned *verb* waved someone over

bizarre *adjective* very strange or unusual

cascading *verb* water falling or pouring down

deafening *adjective* loud

destiny *abstract noun* your destiny is what is intended for you in the future

forecast *verb* predicted

flounder *verb* move clumsily in water

freak *adjective* unusual

frenzy *adjective* not controlled

hunched *adjective* rounded

laden *adjective* carrying something heavy

melancholic *adjective* sad and gloomy

orchard *noun* place where fruit trees are grown

procession *noun* a number of people moving slowly forwards

reef *noun* an area under the sea which is made of rock, coral or sand

shoal *noun* a group of fish

slammed *verb* thrown down with force

somersault *noun* flip over

swollen *adjective* large and rounded

trafficked *verb* illegally bought and sold

trawlers *noun* fishing boats

undergrowth *noun* bushes and other plants growing closely under tall trees

wedged *verb* forced into a narrow space

Key words to help you at school

These words will help you with all your subjects at school.

agree *verb* 1. to think the same as someone

> *Amina says this book is boring, but I don't agree.*

2. to say that you are willing to do something

> *She agreed to show us the way.*

analyse *verb* to examine something carefully

> *This book analyses the causes of the war.*

balance *verb* 1. to remain in a steady position without falling *He balanced on one leg.*

2. to include all the important things in the right amounts *a balanced diet*

balance *noun* the ability to consider every aspect of an issue or situation; fairness

> *Your approach to the situation shows balance.*

bias *noun* a strong feeling in favour of one person or side and against another

> *The referee was accused of bias.*

category *noun* a group or division of similar people or things

> *I'm going to enter the competition in the under-twelves category.*

challenge *verb* to demand someone perform a difficult task or take part in a fight

> *My brother challenged me to a game of darts.*

challenge *noun* something difficult that someone has to do

> *"I accept your challenge," said the knight.*

complex *adjective* 1. made up of many different and connected parts

> *Tropical rainforests are one of the most complex ecosystems on earth.*

2. difficult and complicated

> *She is good at explaining complex ideas in easy language.*

consider *verb* 1. to think carefully about something

> *You should consider the question before you answer it.*

2. to believe something

> *We consider that people should be allowed to follow their own religion.*

consistent *adjective* always the same, regular

> *She's our most consistent player.*

convince *verb* to persuade someone about something

> *My friend convinced me to join the football team.*

critical *adjective* 1. criticising

> *Why do you always have to be so critical?*

2. serious, amounting to a crisis

> *The patient is in a critical condition.*

defend *verb* 1. to protect someone or something from an attack

The villagers defended their homes from the dragon.

2. to argue in support of an idea, belief or person

He defended their right to follow their own religion.

definite *adjective* fixed or certain

Is there a definite date for the party yet?

device *noun* a technique used to produce a particular effect in writing or speech

Rhyme is a common device in poetry.

dispute *noun* a quarrel or disagreement

There was a dispute between the two countries.

verb to argue about something

We dispute their claim.

encourage *verb* to give someone confidence or hope

We were encouraged by all the letters of support.

encourage *verb* 1. to urge someone to do something

My teacher encouraged me to enter the competition.

2. to cause something to develop or increase

Homework encourages self-discipline.

estimate *verb* to make a rough calculation or guess about an amount or value

Can you estimate how long it would take to walk twenty kilometres?

exceptional *adjective* unusual

He showed exceptional talent for art when he was young.

exclude *verb* to keep someone or something out

He was excluded from school.

extract *noun* a piece taken from a book, play or film

Match the story extracts with the illustrations.

extract *verb* to remove something or take it out of something else

Coconut oil is extracted from coconuts.

influence *noun* the power to affect someone or something

He had a huge influence on his younger brother.

influence *verb* to have an effect on what something is or what it does

The tides are influenced by the moon.

instant *adjective* happening immediately

The play has been an instant success.

instant *noun* a moment

I don't believe it for an instant.

logical *adjective* showing clear, step-by-step reasoning; sensible

Are your ideas presented in a logical order?

principal *adjective* chief or most important

Name the principal cities of Australia.

principal *noun* the head of a college or school

The principal congratulated the school's swimming team on winning the cup.

progress *noun* 1. forward movement

The march made slow progress.

2. development or improvement

You have made a lot of progress with your maths.

progress *verb* 1. to move forward

She became more and more tired as the evening progressed.

2. to develop or improve

Technology has progressed steadily in the last twenty years.

project *noun* 1. a planned task in which you find lots out about something and write about it

Pablo chose to do a project about water pollution.

2. a plan or scheme

The school needs to raise money for the building project.

provide *verb* to supply something

A clump of trees provided some welcome shade.

realistic *adjective* 1. true to life

It is a very realistic painting.

2. seeing things as they really are

She is realistic about her chances of winning.

recommend *verb* 1. to suggest something because you think it is good or suitable

I recommend the strawberry ice cream.

2. to advise someone to take action

We recommend that you wear strong shoes on the walk.

refer *verb* to mention someone or something or speak about them

I wasn't referring to you.

relative *adjective* 1. connected or compared with something

the relative sizes of the two cakes

2. compared with the average *They live in relative comfort.*

satisfactory *adjective* 1. good enough

My story was satisfactory.

2. acceptable

He tried to think of a satisfactory explanation.

sequence *noun* 1. a series of things

    We had to do a sequence of exercises.

    2. the order in which things should follow each other

    Arrange the playing cards in sequence, the highest first.

serious *adjective* 1. not funny; important

    I'm not joking – this is serious.

    2. thoughtful or solemn

    His face was serious

    3. very bad

    they've had a serious accident

1 Choose the correct word to complete each sentence.

logical   serious   influence   definite   challenge   critical

a I _____ you to a running race tomorrow!

b Sam was upset when Jen was _____ of her story.

c Are you going to the party or not? Can you give me a
_____ answer?

d Sol's love of pizza will _____ his choice at lunchtime.

e Ben worked through the maths question in a _____
way and found the answer in the end.

f Tash knew she was in _____ trouble when she saw the
broken window.

2 Search for these words.

device   exclude   extract   progress
provide   realistic   refer   sequence

a	r	a	d	p	r	o	v	i	d	e	e
s	e	s	e	o	d	d	l	k	o	n	f
d	a	s	v	s	e	q	u	e	n	c	e
r	l	e	i	f	h	u	k	r	e	o	e
e	i	r	c	i	l	r	x	e	r	r	x
d	s	f	e	x	c	l	u	d	e	d	t
i	t	o	r	d	r	i	e	l	f	i	r
d	i	r	e	e	e	e	r	i	e	e	a
e	c	f	a	x	f	b	p	s	r	r	c
p	r	o	g	r	e	s	s	t	e	e	t
r	x	s	l	c	r	d	o	c	c	c	e
e	e	s	i	t	f	r	s	e	i	e	d

3 Write the words in the correct box.

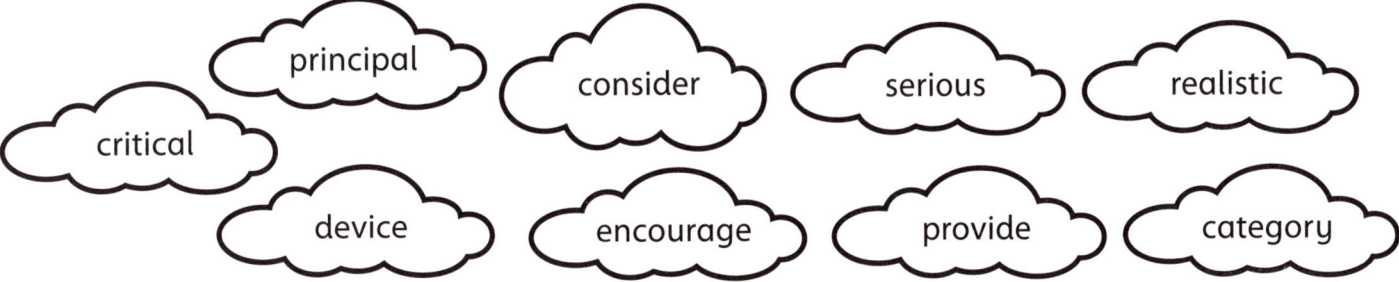

nouns	verbs	adjectives

4 Cross out the word that is the odd one out in each line.

a definite   certain   defend

b estimate   exceptional   guess

c instant   principal   moment

d dispute   logical   reasonable

e sequence   order   complex

f consistent   analyse   examine

5 Draw a line to match each word to its antonym (a word which means the opposite).

dispute	unsatisfactory
encouraging	silly
exceptional	random
exclude	critical
recommend	simple
satisfactory	include
sequence	warn against
serious	agree
complex	ordinary

89

6 Circle the word that has the same meaning as the word in the box.

a balanced

We added weights to each side until the scales were even.

b consistent

Remember to make sure that each letter is a matching size.

c convince

Bao, can you persuade Dishi to come swimming with us?

d project

We all worked together on the task and finished it quickly.

e recommend

Can I suggest that you read this book next?

f relative

I am very short compared to the rest of my family.

7 Write a sentence using each word.

a consider

_____

b complex

_____

c project

_____

d s refer

_____

e instant

_____

f convince

_____

8 Circle the correct word to match the definition.

a protect against attack

defend   encourage   consider

b taking one side over another in an unfair way

device   exclude   bias

c to think about an issue

definite   consider   category

d small part of a story or other text

extract   estimate   exclude

e sub-set of a group

agree   category   device

9 Write a sentence using each word.

a _____

b _____

c _____

d _____

e _____

Grammar and language terms

adjective a word that describes somebody or something

1 *Adjectives* are usually found in front of a noun.
Examples: Green emeralds and **glittering** diamonds.

2 *Adjectives* can also come after a verb.
Examples: It was **big**. They looked **hungry**.

3 Sometimes you can use two *adjectives* together.
Example: tall and handsome
This is called an adjectival phrase.

4 *Adjectives* can be used to describe degrees of intensity. To make a comparative adjective you usually add –*er* (or use more).
Examples: quicker, more beautiful

5 To make a superlative you add –*est* (or use most).
Examples: quickest, most beautiful

adverb a word that describes a verb, or how something was done. Many are formed by adding –*ly* to an *adjective*.
Example: slow/slowly
Adverbs often come next to the verb in a sentence. They can tell the reader:
How something was done: quickly, stupidly, amazingly
Example: She ate her lunch quickly.
Where something happened: there, here, everywhere
Example: After the rainstorm, there was water everywhere.
When something happened: yesterday, today, now
Example: I went to the circus yesterday.
How often something was done: occasionally, often
Example: I visit my grandmother often.

alliteration occurs when two or more nearby words start with the same sound
Example: A slow, sad, sorrowful song.

apostrophe a punctuation mark (') that is used in two ways:

1 To show where letters are missing
Examples: don't (for 'do not'), can't (for 'cannot'), I'm (for 'I am')

2 To show possession
Example: My dog's collar. (This explains that the collar belongs to my dog.)
Example: The boys' cards. (This explains that the cards belong to the boys.)

clause a group of words that contains a subject and a verb. Every full sentence contains at least one main clause.
Example: I ran. (In this clause, 'I' is the subject and 'ran' is the verb.)
Multi-clause sentences contain one or more subordinate clauses. A subordinate clause does not make sense on its own and relies on the main clause.
Example: When I had finished reading it, I returned the book to the library. (In this sentence, the clause 'When I had finished reading it' is a subordinate clause, which depends on the main clause, 'I returned the book to the library' to make sense.)

comma a punctuation mark (,) used to separate parts in a sentence. When you read you must pause briefly where there is a comma. Commas can be used:

1 To separate items in a list
Example: a sunny day, a stretch of sand, several rock pools and an ice-cream van.

2 To place a section of a sentence in parenthesis (as brackets do)
Example: The dog, happy to be outside, was sniffing everything in sight.

3 When addressing someone by name
Example: I understand you, Patricia.

4 After a subordinate clause that starts a sentence
Example: Although it is cold, I am warm.

5 After many connecting conjunctions that we use to start a sentence
Example: However, penguins can get cold…

conjunction a word used to link words or clauses within a sentence
Examples: and, but, so, until, when, as
Example: He was running when he went to the shops.

contraction when an apostrophe is used to show that letters have been removed from a word.
Examples: didn't (for 'did not'), it's (for 'it is')

definition an explanation of the meaning of a word
Example: **purse** a small bag for holding money

dialogue an oral or written conversation

direct speech when speech marks are used to show that someone is speaking.
Example: "Can I talk to you please?" asked Sam.

formal language standard English that we use for school work, official letters and formal settings. In formal language we avoid using contractions, slang words, lots of exclamation marks or capital letters for emphasis.

genre a type of writing.
Examples: poetry, fantasy and non-fiction

homophone one of two or more words that sound the same but have different meanings. They may have the same or different spellings.
Examples: right, write, meat, meet

idiom a colourful expression that cannot be understood from the meaning of its separate words.
Example: It's raining cats and dogs. (This means that it is raining very hard.)

imperative the form of the verb used to make commands.
Example: Go away!

informal language language we use in everyday settings, at home, with friends, via text messages. In writing it includes contractions, slang words and capital letters for emphasis.

metaphor a way of speaking or writing in which one thing is actually said to be something else. This way of speaking or writing is called a figure of speech.
Example: This man is a lion in battle. (This means that he is very brave.)

modal verbs used with a verb to show what is possible, or necessary or what is going to happen.
Example: I **should** go for a run.

narrator the person telling a story

noun a word that names something or somebody
Examples: fox, chicken, brother, rock
Nouns can be singular (dog) or plural (dogs).
A *collective noun* refers to a group.
Example: a **flock** of birds
A *proper noun* begins with a capital letter and names a person, a place or something specifically.
Examples: Mrs Brown, London

paragraph a group of sentences that a piece of writing is divided into. Each *paragraph* begins on a new line.

personification the technique of giving human qualities to things that are not human, such as an animal, concept or inanimate object.
Example: The sun beamed happily while the kittens played hide-and-seek, and life danced by.

phrase a small group of words that forms part of a clause. Phrases do not make sense on their own.

plot what happens in a story, film or play

prefix a word or syllable placed at the beginning of a word to modify its meaning.
Examples: In the word 'misunderstand', the prefix *mis–* makes the word 'understand' mean 'not understand correctly'. In the word 'unhappy', the prefix *un–* makes the word 'happy' mean 'not happy'.

preposition a word that indicates place (on, in), direction (over, beyond) or time (during, on) among others.
Examples: I put the book **in** the drawer. I read my book **during** lunch.

pronoun a word that can replace a noun
Examples: I, me, mine, myself

reported speech when you report someone's words in a changed form.
Example: "I am at home." (direct speech)
She said she was at home. (reported speech)

rhyme when the endings of words sound similar
Example: **bat** and **mat**, **batter** and **matter**

rhythm a regular pattern of beats in poetry

sentence a group of words that expresses a complete thought. All sentences begin with a capital letter and end with a full stop, question mark or exclamation mark. There are four types of sentences:

1 Statements – that declare something and end in a full stop (.).
   Example: The class yelled in triumph.
2 Questions – that ask something and end in a question mark (?).
   Example: Where is the dog?
3 Exclamations – that exclaim and end in an exclamation mark (!).
   Example: I'm so tired!
4 Imperatives – that command or instruct and can end either in a full stop or an exclamation mark.
   Example: Put on your coat right away!

Single-clause sentences are made up of one clause.
Example: I am hungry.
Multi-clause sentences are made up of two or more main clauses, usually joined by a conjunction.
Example: I am hungry and I am thirsty.

simile a figure of speech in which two things are compared using the linking words 'like' or 'as'
Example: In battle, he was as brave as a lion.

singular/plural *singular* refers to one thing and *plural* refers to more than one thing.
Examples:
dog (singular)   dogs (plural)
sky (singular)   skies (plural)
wolf (singular)   wolves (plural)

sub-heading comes below a heading and indicates to the reader the contents of smaller units of text

subordinate clause See *clause*

suffix a word or syllable placed at the end of a word to modify its meaning
Example: In the word 'tasteless' the suffix –*less* makes the word 'tasteless' mean 'with no taste'.

superlative See *adjective*

syllable a unit of pronunciation that forms part of or the whole of a word. English words consist of one or more syllables. Each syllable always contains one speech vowel. This may have one or more speech consonants before and/or after it.
Examples: 1 syllable - house, 2 syllables - kettle, 3 syllables - butterfly

synonym a word or phrase that means exactly or nearly the same as another word or phrase in the same language.
Example: *Shut* is a synonym of *close*.

tense a verb form that shows whether events happen in the past, present or the future.
Examples:
The Pyramids are on the west bank of the River Nile. (present tense)
They were built as enormous tombs. (past tense)
They will stand for centuries to come. (future tense)
Most verbs change their spelling by adding –*ed* to form the **past tense**.
Example: walk/walked
Some have irregular spellings.
Example: catch/caught
Most verbs use 'will' to form the **future tense**.
Example: I will go to school tomorrow.

verb shows the action in a sentence and can express a process or state

1 *Verbs* are often known as 'doing', 'being', 'action' or 'happening' words.
   Example: The boys **run** down the hill.
   (In this sentence the word 'run' is the *verb*.)
2 Sometimes several words make up the *verb*.
   Example: The boys **are running**.
   (In this case *running* is the main verb and *are* is an extra verb that adds to the meaning. It is called an *auxiliary verb*.)

vowel is one of the five letters in writing **a**, **e**, **i**, **o** or **u**. In speech, a *vowel* is a sound made with the mouth open and the airway unobstructed. Each syllable in a word has one *vowel* sound.

Oxford International Primary

English
Workbook

6

Emma Danihel

OXFORD

Great Clarendon Street, Oxford, OX2 6DP, United Kingdom

Oxford University Press is a department of the University of Oxford. It furthers the University's objective of excellence in research, scholarship, and education by publishing worldwide. Oxford is a registered trade mark of Oxford University Press in the UK and in certain other countries

British Library Cataloguing in Publication Data

Data available

978-1-38-202013-8

10 9 8 7 6 5 4

Paper used in the production of this book is a natural, recyclable product made from wood grown in sustainable forests. The manufacturing process conforms to the environmental regulations of the country of origin.

Printed in India by Manipal Technologies Limited

Acknowledgements

The publisher and authors would like to thank the following for permission to use photographs and other copyright material:

Cover: Artwork by Dan Gartman. **Photos: p3(a):** James Devaney/Getty Images; **p3(b):** Smileus/Shutterstock; **p3(c):** Jaroslav Moravcik/Shutterstock; **p6(tr):** artshock/Shutterstock; **p8(bl):** Maryline/Shuttertstock; **p14:** Shahjehan/Shutterstock; **p13:** oxanakot/Shutterstock; **p12(m):** Laurent Lairys/Agence Locevaphotos / Alamy Stock Photo; **p17(m):** Churovskaya Sofia/Shutterstock; **p18(br):** John1179/Shutterstock; **p26(tr):** KatBranchArt/Shutterstock; **p21(tr):** Helen Stebakov/Shutterstock; **p33(m):** AcantStudio/Shutterstock; **p34(tr):** oguz senoguz/Shutterstock; **p36(tr):** robuart/Shutterstock; **p36(br):** Nickimpression/Shutterstock; **p38(mr):** olegganko/Shutterstock; **p39(br):** Nataliia Pavliuk/Shutterstock; **p40(br):** sharpner/Shutterstock; **p44:** Kakigori Studio/Shutterstock; **p46(tr):** Aluna1/Shutterstock; **p48(t-b):** Light-Dew/Shutterstock; **p49(mr):** Farferros/Shutterstock; **p50:** kornn/Shutterstock; **p54(m):** Reamolko/Shutterstock; **p55(m):** TheModernCanvas/Shutterstock; **p56(br):** Lulupainting/Shutterstock; **p57(tr):** Kheng Guan Toh/Shutterstock; **p63(tr):** Alexander_P/Shutterstock; **p64(m):** Jekaterina V/Shutterstock; **p66(bl-br):** Ku_suriuri/Shutterstock; **p68(tr-br):** cosmaa/Shutterstock; **p73(tr):** Nature Art/Shutterstock; **p74(tr):** Katerina Kreker/Shutterstock.

Artwork by Dan Gartman, Alfredo Belli, Nina Caniac, Stefan Chabluk, Katriona Chapman, Russ Daff, Jacqui Davis, Dylan Gibson, Alan Marks, Mel Matthews, Gustavo Mazali, Simon Mendes, Dusan Pavlic, Claudia Ranucci, Francesca Resta, Giulia Rivolta, Kimberley Scott, Meilo So, Mike Spoor, Mark Walker, Jan Wijngaard, and Claudia Venturini, Scott Plumbe, OKS Group, Andy Parker/Oxford University Press, and Q2A Media Services Pvt. Ltd.

Dave Calder: 'Flood' from *Dolphins Leap Lampposts* poems by Dave Calder, Eric Finney and Ian Souter (Macmillan, 2002). © Dave Calder 1989. Reproduced with permission from D. Calder.

John Foster: 'The Price of Fame' from *The Poetry Chest* (Oxford University Press, 2007). Reproduced with permission from Oxford University Press.

Elizabeth Laird: Pulling Together from *Why Dogs Have Black Noses* (Oxford Reading Tree, Myths and Legends, Oxford University Press, 2010). Reproduced with permission from Oxford University Press.

Spike Milligan: 'The ABC' from *Silly Verse for Kids* (Penguin, 1968). Reproduced with permission from Spike Milligan Productions Ltd.

Any third party use of this material, outside of this publication, is prohibited. Interested parties should apply to the copyright holders indicated in each case.

Although we have made every effort to trace and contact all copyright holders before publication this has not been possible in all cases. If notified, the publisher will rectify any errors or omissions at the earliest opportunity.